The Portrait of a Virtuous Woman

Finding Your Freedom in God's Perfect Plan for You

Taffi L. Dollar

Publishers Since 1798

THOMAS NELSON PUBLISHERS®
Nashville

A Division of Thomas Nelson, Inc.
www.ThomasNelson.com

Published in Nashville, Tennessee, by Thomas Nelson, Inc.

Unless otherwise noted, Scripture quotations are from the KING JAMES VERSION of the Bible.

Scripture quotations noted NKJV are from THE NEW KING JAMES VERSION. Copyright © 1979, 1980, 1982, Thomas Nelson, Inc., Publishers.

Scripture quotations noted AMPLIFIED are from THE AMPLIFIED BIBLE: Old Testament. Copyright © 1962, 1964 by Zondervan Publishing House (used by permission); and from THE AMPLIFIED NEW TESTAMENT. Copyright © 1958 by the Lockman Foundation (used by permission).

ISBN 0-7852-6310-1

Library of Congress Cataloging-in-Publication Data

Previously published as A *Woman After God's Own Heart*

Printed in the United States of America.
05 RRD 5 4

Contents

This book is dedicated to my mother, Ethel Bolton. You have been my greatest inspiration, and because of you, I have become the woman that I am. Despite the oppositions you have faced in life, your strength, determination, and fortitude have propelled you to new heights, greater faith, and unwavering confidence in God. Thanks for never giving up!

Mom, you are a tremendous inspiration to my family, and we are so grateful to have you in our lives. You are truly a woman, wife, mother, grandmother, and friend after God's own heart.

I love you!
Taffi

Introduction

The character of a virtuous woman is influenced, tempered, and fashioned by the Word of God. She is a woman—married or single—who places God above everything and everyone in her life by making His Word the final authority in all that she does. A virtuous woman has the mind of Christ, and she reflects His image. She has learned, through submission to God and to His Word, how to live free from stress and how to walk in His perfect will. In essence, she pleases God.

Becoming a virtuous woman requires a commitment to becoming whole through His Word. This is not something that can be accomplished by watching soap operas or reading secular magazines. It cannot be accomplished overnight. Learning to operate with the mind of Christ is an ongoing process that involves spending time with God and basking in His presence continually—seeking Him for direction at every turn.

My prayer is that you will use the information in this book to supplement your time with God. As you read the Scriptures and say the confession given in each chapter, I encourage you to make a quality decision to become all that you can be for God, your family, and yourself. Allow the Word of God to settle in your spirit. It will propel you to a new level of living and thinking, and it will change your life forever!

*A capable, intelligent, and virtuous woman—
who is he who can find her?*

Proverbs 31:10, AMPLIFIED

1

The Virtuous Woman

~——~

GOD HAS CALLED US TO BE WOMEN OF VIRTUE. "But what exactly does that mean?" you may ask. It simply means that God wants us to live in the power and anointing of His strength rather than our own. However, most of us are accustomed to doing just the opposite. The virtue found in God provides us with everything we need—righteousness, strength, ability, and anointing. These attributes instill in us a strong sense of value and spiritual excellence.

Godly character is beneficial not only to

> Godly character is beneficial not only to us, but also to others.

us, but also to others. It radiates light to those who live in darkness and edifies those who are in the body of Christ. The truth of the matter is that God blesses us so that we may be a blessing to others (Gen. 12:3). He expects us to use what He has given us to have a positive effect on them. Everything God does is done with a purpose. Everything you will ever need in life has already been given to you. The Scriptures say He has given to us "all things that pertain unto life and godliness, through the knowledge of him that hath called us to glory and virtue" (2 Peter 1:3).

God has called us to glory and virtue. *Glory* is "the manifested Word of God." It is the reality of what God says, and His divine plan is that we walk in it every single day. According to Scripture, God has also called us to walk in virtue. In other words, He has called us to walk in the power of His might.

"I Shall Be Whole"

Remember the woman with the issue of blood? She had been hemorrhaging for twelve years. After going to several doctors and taking all kinds of medicine, she still had the problem. As a matter of fact, her condition grew worse. When she heard that Jesus was nearby, she confessed her healing by speaking these words: "If I may touch but his clothes, I shall be whole" (Mark 5:28). Right away, the woman was healed. Just think, for years she sought medical treatment for the same problem and was never healed.

However, she received immediate results when she touched Jesus and opened her mouth to confess her deliverance! She acted on what she believed. That's what *faith* is—"acting on the Word of God." The Word also says, "Add to your faith virtue; and to virtue knowledge" (2 Peter 1:5). "And Jesus, immediately knowing in himself that virtue had gone out of him, turned him about in the press, and said, Who touched my clothes?" (Mark 5:30).

You see, the virtue in Jesus, coupled with her own faith, made the woman whole. Virtue came out of Jesus and went into her. God always delivers us *out of* one thing *into* something else. The woman was not only healed; she was made *whole* or "complete" (Mark 5:34). It's quite clear then that we also must tap into the power that God has given us to become complete in Him. And isn't it good to know that we can be made whole, and that every broken piece in our lives can be healed? Honey, there is no need for us to continue to live with broken hearts, painful memories, sickness, or even regret. There is nothing lacking in God's provision. If God could make that woman whole after twelve years of suffering, He can do the same for you and me. According to the writer of Hebrews, "Jesus Christ is the same yesterday, today, and forever" (13:8 NKJV). God has already given you all things. Your job is to believe and lay hold of them.

Once you begin to trust in God's ability to make you whole, you will be able to let go of some of the thoughts and feelings that have held you back from walking in the fullness God created you to walk in. The Word of God says to "lay aside every weight" (Heb. 12:1 NKJV). There is no need to hold on to anything that God can erase or make new again. I encourage you to examine your heart, and if you're holding on to any issue that is contrary to God's promises, give it to God and let it go. Here's what I mean.

If the doctor says that he can treat your illness but he can't cure it, give it to God. If your friends tell you that you'll never love again or that there's no solution for your rocky marriage except divorce, give it to God. If anyone tells you that you'll be in debt for the rest of your life, and that you'll never have the home or lifestyle you desire, give it to God. You see, the woman's issue of blood represented a concern in her life that seemed hopeless. After going here and there, trying to remedy her problem, she found that the only permanent solution was Jesus. Her confession confirmed that fact. In essence, she said, "As soon as I touch Jesus, I'll be finished with this thing forever!" The same is true for you. As soon as you tap into God's virtue and learn to rely more on Him than on yourself, the issue in your life will greatly diminish.

A Woman of Excellence

Now let's consider the distinct character portrayed by a woman of virtue. She is a lady in every sense of the word: honorable, truthful, and confident. She represents excellence and is anointed to get the job done. The example is given in Proverbs 31:

A capable, intelligent, and virtuous woman—who is he who can find her? She is far more precious than jewels and her value is far above rubies or pearls. The heart of her husband trusts in her confidently and relies on and believes in her securely, so that he has no lack of [honest] gain or need of [dishonest] spoil. She comforts, encourages, and does him only good as long as there is life within her . . . She rises while it is yet night and gets [spiritual] food for her household and assigns her maids their tasks. She considers a [new] field before she buys or accepts it [expanding prudently and not courting neglect of her present duties by assuming other duties]; with her savings [of time and strength] she plants fruitful vines in her vineyard. She girds herself with strength [spiritual, mental, and physical fitness for her God-given task] and makes her arms strong and firm. She tastes and sees that her gain from work [with and for God] is good . . . She opens her hand to the poor, yes, she reaches out her filled hands to the needy [whether in body, mind, or spirit] . . . Her husband is known in the [city's] gates, when he sits among the elders of the land . . . Strength and dignity are her clothing and her position is strong and secure; she rejoices over the future [the latter day or time to come, knowing that she and her family are in readiness for it]! She opens her mouth in skillful and godly Wisdom, and on her tongue is the law of kindness [giving counsel and instruction]. She looks well to how things go in her household, and the bread of idleness (gossip, discontent, and self-pity) she will not eat. Her children rise up and call her blessed (happy, fortunate, and to be envied); and her husband boasts of and praises her, [saying], Many daughters have done virtuously, nobly, and well [with the strength of character that is steadfast in goodness], but you excel them all. Charm and grace are deceptive, and beauty is vain [because it is not lasting], but a woman who reverently and worshipfully fears the Lord, she shall be praised! (vv. 10–12, 15–18, 20, 23, 25–30 AMPLIFIED)

God has given us this model to follow to become virtuous women. As you can see, this woman of God is anointed. She relies on God's unlimited strength and power rather than her own. A virtuous woman is confident, intelligent, and supportive. She is also mentally, spiritually, and physically fit. The well-being of her household is her primary focus, and she is careful not to overextend herself by getting too involved in ventures outside the home that may cause her family to

> *The woman of God is anointed. She relies on God's unlimited strength and power rather than her own.*

suffer. The virtuous woman is prosperous and wealthy, and her husband is known throughout the city. This woman blesses the poor and exercises godly wisdom. She neither initiates nor listens to gossip. She isn't lazy.

You may be saying, "Does it take all that to be considered virtuous?" I'll say this: if God said it, it can be done. Now don't get me wrong. I'm not totally there yet, but it is my goal to get there. We may look at all the things the virtuous woman does and think, *That's impossible in this day and time. All that sewing of tapestry and planting of gardens.* I don't know about all this. To be absolutely honest, I was initially a bit skeptical myself. For a long time, I heard and read this Scripture without full understanding. To me, the virtuous woman was a person who seemed unrealistic. You know what I mean? Her character seemed impossible to develop. But it's not.

Over the years, I've learned that the best thing to do is to jot down a list of the characteristics found in Proverbs 31, pick a place to start, and just begin. No one is asking you to sew! Find out what you're anointed to do well and excel at it. Set your heart on the goal as Paul did in Philippians 3:13–14: "I count not myself to have apprehended: but this one thing I do, forgetting those things which are behind, and reaching forth unto those things which are before, I press toward the mark for the prize of the high calling of God in Christ Jesus."

Child of God, great things have been prepared for you and me. And the only way to withdraw the virtue needed to accomplish our goals is to tap into the source that produces virtue—the Word of God. We've got to be willing with gladness of heart to do what God says. It's like losing weight. If you're like me, you're not all that excited about getting up early to do squats and sit-ups. But once you begin to see the results, you get over it because the benefits outweigh the challenge.

A Godly Woman's Character

My husband, Creflo, often teaches on the characteristics that a godly woman should possess—and with good reason. There are many women who make decisions based more on worldly values than on the Word of God. They also struggle with their self-image, which may lead to a seemingly never-ending cycle of poor decisions.

A few things that come to mind from my husband's teachings on character include relationships, appropriate dress, and personality. Relationships are an important part of a woman's life. They generally involve people and issues that are close to the heart. Many times we allow our relationships to dictate our actions and responses rather than allow God to have total control.

There are three types of relationships: outer-court, inner-court, and the Holiest of Holies. Outer-court relationships include acquaintances; inner-court relationships include close friends. However, the people in your Holiest of Holies know your innermost secrets and desires. Very few people should be allowed here. In fact, only your spouse, family, and closest friends should know you that well. As a woman of God, you should choose your friends carefully. Select those who have similar beliefs, values, and standards, and those who live according to the Word of God.

I may be treading on thin ice when I approach the topic of appropriate dress, but I have to be straight with you. A woman of God simply can't wear certain clothes—for instance, blouses that show too much cleavage, skirts that show too much leg, and what have you. You know what I mean—wearing jeans that are so tight, you have to lie down and suck in your stomach just to zip them. Save clothes that are revealing for your husband's eyes only—not your boyfriend's and definitely not a stranger's. A lot of women get off track here and fall into situations that should never happen.

My husband helped me in the area of appropriate dress when we were dating. I thought, *If you've got it, flaunt it, and the tighter the better.* At first, I was offended when he began to talk to me about my standard of dress. I thought, *Who does he think he is?* But as I began to seek God's Word for wisdom, I realized that he was right. Deep inside, I wanted to please God more than anything. I also wanted to please Creflo and make him proud.

There is absolutely nothing wrong with looking your best. A woman of God can dress fashionably and sensibly without conforming to the world's way of dressing. Just keep in mind that you're a godly woman, and you represent the King and His kingdom. God is creative and so are you. Create your own style; be as sharp as you like. God has no problem with your looking good.

But no amount of looking good will cover up a personality that needs work. For example, a loud woman is not a good representation of a virtuous woman. The Word calls that kind of woman "foolish . . . clamorous . . . simple" (Prov. 9:13). It goes on to say that the foolish woman knows nothing. She is viewed as silly. If you're loud, tone down a bit. Don't scream across the parking lot! Conduct yourself appropriately. Be someone God can be proud of. A virtuous woman conducts herself in a way that glorifies God. Whether or not you

> *Your life should reflect God's goodness and His abundant blessings.*

have a husband, you are far more attractive when you choose to use gentle words and demonstrate kind behavior. Remember that true beauty comes from within.

If you desire to walk in the strength, power, and anointing of a virtuous woman, the Word of God must be evident in your daily living. The truth of God's promises must be visible to all. Your life should reflect God's goodness and His abundant blessings. The Word of God assures us that He "is able to do exceeding abundantly above all that we ask or think, according to the power that worketh in us" (Eph. 3:20).

Our Resources

The power that works in us is made available by God through several resources. One is the Holy Spirit, who dwells within the inner man. He has been appointed by God to lead us into all truth (John 16:13). The Holy Spirit is also our Comforter, Friend, and Counselor (John 14:18). Tapping into the Holy Spirit as a resource increases strength and develops the character of Christ within us. The Holy Spirit knows the mind of Christ. He is trustworthy, dependable, and always available. Begin to recognize Him for who He is, and take advantage of the added power God has given you by allowing the Holy Spirit to work on your behalf.

Jesus also lives inside us. All too often we forget that, so let me say it again: Jesus—your ultimate Source of power—lives inside you! He sees all, feels all, and hears all. Jesus' goal on earth was to please the Father. He said, "For I always do those things that please Him" (John 8:29 NKJV). Likewise, your goal should be to please God.

You please God when you obey His voice and do what He says to do. There are several ways to accomplish this goal. First, read and obey the written Word of God. Second, learn to hear the voice of God when He speaks to your spirit. From time to time, you may find yourself saying, "Something told me not to do that." It's not *something*, Child of God. It's God speaking to your spirit.

James spoke this truth: "If any of you lack wisdom, let him ask of God, that giveth to all men liberally . . . and it shall be given him" (James 1:5). Ask God how to please Him. Ask Him to reveal to you His perfect will. He promises that you will receive wisdom when you ask.

Don't fall into the trap of being content with where you are. Instead, stretch to the next level! Don't try to look, sound, or live like the world. Separate yourself from that old way of life, and tap into the strength and power found in God's Word so that you may fulfill His purpose for your life.

Confession

I am a virtuous woman. I am capable, intelligent, trustworthy, dependable, and supportive. I am clothed with strength and dignity. I am anointed. I am an excellent representation of Christ in my relationships, my dress, the words I speak, and my total being. According to the Word of God, I have all things that pertain to life and godliness. Jesus and the Holy Spirit dwell in me; therefore, I am equipped to carry out God's purpose for my life. I declare this to be so now in Jesus' name. Amen.

Study Questions

1. How sure are you that God can count on you to obey Him?

2. Does God have a place of priority in your day, or are you fitting Him in?

3. How much of your time is spent on responsibilities and activities outside your home? Does this take away from time spent with your family?

4. Is the well-being of your family your primary focus? If so, how do you demonstrate your commitment to placing them first?

5. In what areas of your life are you operating in your human strength rather than in God's strength?

6. How much effort do you put into becoming physically beautiful? Do you work just as hard at becoming spiritually beautiful?

7. Are you content with where you are in life as a woman of God, or are you willing to stretch to the next level of growth?

8. Which of the character traits mentioned in Proverbs 31 have you mastered? Which ones need improvement?

Challenge

Make a list of the areas in your life where you are operating in human strength rather than in God's strength. Ask God to teach you how to tap into His supply of anointing so that you may become fully equipped with His power.

Fill up and complete my joy by living in harmony and being of the same mind and one in purpose, having the same love, being in full accord and of one harmonious mind and intention. Do nothing from factional motives [through contentiousness, strife, selfishness, or for unworthy ends] or prompted by conceit and empty arrogance. Instead, in the true spirit of humility (lowliness of mind) let each regard the others as better than and superior to himself [thinking more highly of one another than you do of yourselves]. Let each of you esteem and look upon and be concerned for not [merely] his own interests, but also each for the interests of others. Let this same attitude and purpose and [humble] mind be in you which was in Christ Jesus: [Let Him be your example in humility].

—Philippians 2:2–5 AMPLIFIED

2

Having the Mind of Christ

~

AS CHRISTIANS, WE MUST FOLLOW THE EXAMPLE SET BY Christ. This opening passage of Scripture clearly outlines the "mind," or the "attitude," we are to reflect. When we line ourselves up according to God's Word, we position ourselves to receive His blessings. Remember, our goal should always be the same as Jesus'—to please the Father.

Although this may not be the easiest thing to do, I assure you it can be done. The information in this chapter may be hard on your flesh because it deals with areas of sensitivity, which include selfishness, pride, insecurity, and inadequacy. You may become uncomfortable or even slightly offended—but don't be. The benefits that come from exposing and dealing with these issues will far outweigh any feelings of offense.

Humility

The primary attribute in Jesus' character was *humility*. While on earth He purposely decided to think more highly of others than Himself. In other words, He put their needs before His. Here is an example that may bring this idea closer to home. In marriage, if each person puts the needs of the other first, ultimately both will be happy. Why?

> *In marriage, if each person puts the needs of the other first, ultimately both will be happy.*

When your needs are met, you are more apt to meet the needs of your spouse and vice versa. Without so many words your actions say, "Treat me nice, and I'll treat you nice." But oftentimes, we cop an attitude when our needs are unmet because in our opinion what is being done is not sufficient. It would be better in this case to take a closer look at yourself and see if you're giving your partner what you expect to receive. How well are you meeting his needs? You may find that you, too, need to work harder to please your mate.

Your attitude indicates your ability to perform, and it determines how successful you will be—in your job, in your relationships, and in your service to God. The way that you approach a situation determines how well things will turn out. Your attitude determines whether you choose to be positive and believe God for the best in each circumstance or whether you operate in a negative state of mind and take on a spirit of fear.

Attitude is "an inward choice or decision that is expressed outwardly." No one can force you to have a bad attitude. It's a choice. For instance, I *choose* to be happy, sad, lovable, or hateful. Attitudes don't just happen. They are often influenced by the way you think and feel. For this reason, it is best to choose the attitude of Christ.

Did you know that a good attitude will take you farther than your ability? Sometimes when I'm hiring new employees, I am inclined to choose the person who demonstrates the best attitude rather than the one with the best record of ability. I believe that if a person chooses to live with a good attitude, he or she can use that strength to believe God for the ability that's needed to get the job done.

Your *disposition* or "personality" reveals a lot about you. You can look at the people around you and discern their attitudes. Try it. Look at your neighbor, coworker, children, or spouse. See what I mean? It's the same when they look at you. They can determine just by looking at your expressions and by observing your behavior what type of attitude you have.

Now let's take a closer look at Jesus:

Who, although being essentially one with God and in the form of God [possessing the fullness of the attributes which make God God], did not think this equality with God was a thing to be eagerly grasped or retained, but stripped Himself [of all privileges and rightful dignity], so as to assume the guise of a servant (slave), in that He became like men and was born a human being. And after He had appeared in human form, He abased and humbled Himself [still further] and carried His obedience to the extreme of death, even the death of the cross! (Phil. 2:6–8 AMPLIFIED)

Although He was God and was anointed to do everything His Father said, He chose to live as humans do. Because of Jesus' decision to live this way in order to fulfill the will of the Father, God exalted Him. Read these verses where Paul encouraged us to judge ourselves and to become Christlike:

Therefore, my dear ones, as you have always obeyed [my suggestions], so now, not only [with the enthusiasm you would show] in my presence but much more because I am absent, work out (cultivate, carry out to the goal, and fully complete) your own salvation with reverence and awe and trembling (self-distrust, with serious caution,

tenderness of conscience, watchfulness against temptation, timidly shrinking from whatever might offend God
and discredit the name of Christ). [Not in your own
strength] for it is God Who is all the while effectually at
work in you [energizing and creating in you the power
and desire], both to will and to work for His good pleasure and satisfaction and delight. Do all things without
grumbling and faultfinding and complaining [against
God] and questioning and doubting [among yourselves],
that you may show yourselves to be blameless and guile-
less, innocent and uncontaminated, children of God
without blemish (faultless, unrebukable) in the midst of
a crooked and wicked generation [spiritually perverted
and perverse], among whom you are seen as bright lights
(stars or beacons shining out clearly) in the [dark] world.
(Phil. 2:12–15 AMPLIFIED)

Paul also admonished us to keep our attitudes in check by
making the change without grumbling or complaining,
relying instead on God's strength rather than our own.

Servant Spirit

Another strong characteristic in Jesus was His *willingness to take on the spirit of a servant.* He was willing to do
whatever needed to be done. Can God count on you to do

whatever it takes, despite the cost? Jesus yielded and submitted to God's plan and purpose. Despite persecution, He always managed to maintain a good attitude.

A bad attitude is the result of selfish will. Generally this thought prevails: *Things have to go my way.* Personally, I had a challenge with this one. I remember growing up and often hearing my dad say, "You have such a bad attitude." I didn't understand what he meant. When I married Creflo, he began to say the same thing. Later, I began to realize that my attitude was a result of my selfish will.

Sometimes people get divorced because of their bad attitude, which may be the result of unforgiveness, hurt, selfishness, or fear. Their reactions are often based upon how they are treated or how they feel. Many times offense is the root cause of our actions.

At some point, I learned that God could use me more effectively if I would be willing to change. As a result, I changed my attitude concerning everything in life—my marriage, my position in ministry, even exercise. In fact, I had to change my attitude about the treadmill. (Rather than being my worst enemy, it has become my best friend.) I also had to learn to be less critical of others and not look at things from a negative perspective. It's a process that I'm still working on. But it's a decision that I've decided to stick with in order to get to the place where God has called me to be.

Jesus would never have been able to fulfill His call with a bad attitude. The same is true for us. Since our call is

> *We, too, must work toward and maintain a good attitude.*

to fulfill the Father's will for our lives, we, too, must work toward and maintain a good attitude.

Let's look at two examples in the Bible regarding attitude. The first concerns a Pharisee and a publican (a tax collector):

> And he spake this parable unto certain which trusted in themselves that they were righteous, and despised others: Two men went up into the temple to pray; the one a Pharisee, and the other a publican. The Pharisee stood and prayed thus with himself, God, I thank thee, that I am not as other men are, extortioners, unjust, adulterers, or even as this publican. I fast twice in the week, I give tithes of all that I possess. And the publican, standing afar off, would not lift up so much as his eyes unto heaven, but smote upon his breast, saying, God be merciful to me a sinner. (Luke 18:9–13)

Do you think God was more pleased with the publican or the Pharisee? The Scripture reveals in verse 14 that God was more pleased with the publican: "For every one that exalteth himself shall be abased; and he that humbleth himself shall be exalted."

The second example is the life of Joseph, who demonstrated humility and a good attitude. Despite his brothers' betrayal, Joseph exhibited the attitude of Christ in many circumstances. They sold him into slavery when he was young. Nonetheless, because of his good attitude, God showered him with favor and blessings. His story is quite interesting, and I encourage you to read it (Gen. 37–50).

This part of the story picks up when Joseph was older and had been made ruler over Egypt. There was famine in the land, and his brothers, like many others, came to Joseph for food. He was their only hope for obtaining food. Because Joseph pleased God, he abounded with blessings and was not affected by famine. As a matter of fact, he had enough to go around. His brothers had no idea that he was the brother they had sold into slavery so many years before.

> And Joseph said unto his brethren, Come near to me, I pray you. And they came near. And he said, I am Joseph your brother, whom ye sold into Egypt. Now therefore be not grieved, nor angry with yourselves, that ye sold me hither: for God did send me before you to preserve [your] life . . . And God sent me before you to preserve you a posterity in the earth, and to save your lives by a great deliverance. (Gen. 45:4–5, 7)

Look at that! Joseph not only forgave them, but he also pleaded with them not to feel guilty for their actions. Then he gave them everything they needed to prosper and live well. Glory to God! If Joseph could do that, surely you and I can stand a little attitude adjustment in facing our trials. Although we may have been betrayed in the past or hurt by family members, I don't think any of us have been sold into slavery. Joseph's story should encourage and inspire us.

Security

Let's return to the life of Jesus. A third characteristic demonstrated in His life was *security*. Jesus was very secure. He never felt the need to prove Himself to anyone. When the devil tried to provoke Him to demonstrate His power and authority, Jesus refused (Matt. 4:1–11). And so it should be with us. We don't need to go around proving ourselves to others or feeling

> *I know whose I am, and who I am is determined by what the Word of God says about me.*

inadequate. Jesus is a child of the King, and so are you. Just knowing that you are God's child should increase your confidence.

I don't have time to worry about what people think of me. I've been there and done that. I know whose I am, and *who* I am is determined by what the Word of God says about me. It says that I am *blessed,* which means I am "empowered to prosper." It says that I am healed because by the stripes of Jesus I am already healed (Isa. 53:5; 1 Peter 2:24). It says that I have angels to protect me wherever I go (Ps. 91:11–12). The Word of God says that I have the power to move mountains in my life (Matt. 17:20), and that includes debt, depression, strife, jealousy, and fear. It even says that I am forgiven as soon as I repent (1 John 1:9). Child of God, there is no reason to feel insecure in who you are. You're the King's kid, and you have nothing to prove. The Word of God speaks for itself. If you're having a challenge in this area, believe what God says about you and forget the rest.

Submission

The fourth attribute demonstrated in the life of Jesus was another difficult area for me—*submission.* For a long time I thought God had something against women. I cringed when I heard the word *submission,* particularly as it relates to marriage. However, I had to learn the true meaning of submission. I have learned that submission is for everyone, and it must be demonstrated first and foremost to

God. I'll talk more about submission and my personal experiences later.

Jesus illustrated the best example for us in His submission to God. He was not rebellious, and He made Himself of no reputation for our benefit. In the Greek, that literally means He emptied Himself. He dumped everything out from the beginning: His deity, privileges—everything. No one took it from Him; instead, He willingly released it all. His concern was for us, not Himself. He came so that we might have life and life more abundantly (John 10:10). Think for a moment: How willing are you to lay aside your plans to become submitted to God's will?

Oftentimes when we are offended or betrayed, we want to tell the person off. But we can learn a lot from Jesus' response when Judas betrayed Him with a kiss:

> But Jesus said to him, "Friend, why have you come?" Then they came and laid hands on Jesus and took Him. And suddenly, one of those who were with Jesus stretched out his hand and drew his sword, struck the servant of the high priest, and cut off his ear. But Jesus said to him, "Put your sword in its place, for all who take the sword will perish by the sword. Or do you think that I cannot now pray to My Father, and He will provide Me with more than twelve legions of angels? How then could the Scriptures be fulfilled, that it must happen thus?" (Matt. 26:50–54 NKJV)

While Jesus recognized the authority given Him by the Father, He also knew the right time to use it. Timing is important because sometimes our response becomes the deciding factor in the outcome. Although God has given us the power and authority to do certain things, we have to be amenable to His timing. Had Jesus used His authority in that situation, He would have forfeited the Father's will for us to receive salvation.

Jesus' response was based on His calling and purpose, not His ability. Likewise, we must be careful that bad attitudes don't rise up in us when we are mistreated. Decide that you will overcome the temptation to "snap" or "go off" when you are tried; rather, submit to

> *Begin to operate with the mind of Christ.*

the will of the Father. Stay in control of the situation. Don't allow circumstances to move you. Remember your calling and purpose. You have all that you need to fulfill your purpose and get the job done. Begin to operate with the mind of Christ.

Confession

Heavenly Father, I renounce every bad attitude that I've had concerning You, other people, and Your Word. I repent now, and I thank You that I have the mind of Christ. I humble myself by esteeming others higher than myself. I will not allow situations to control me. I make a decision to always have a good attitude in everything. I will adjust my attitude to line up with Your Word. Isaiah 26:3 says, "Thou wilt keep him in perfect peace, whose mind is stayed on thee: because he trusteth in thee." I trust You, Lord, and I know that Your Word is true. Thank You for perfecting the things that concern me (Ps. 138:8). I live to fulfill Your desire for my life; therefore, I submit to Your will. I will not let any person, situation, or thing determine how I respond because I am full of and controlled by the Holy Spirit. I declare this to be so now in Jesus' name. Amen.

Study Questions

1. What experiences, people, or fears have influenced the attitude in which you operate?

2. Do you consider others first, or does your personal agenda come first?

3. Can people determine by your attitude that you are a child of God, or is your Christianity evident only in the Christian materials you display?

4. Are you able to maintain a good attitude when you are mistreated? If so, how? If not, how can you improve?

5. Can you honestly say that your general attitude reflects the mind of Christ? If so, what evidence in your life proves this to be true?

6. How often do you seek God for direction in handling personal issues?

7. How much faith do you have in God's ability to perfect those things that concern you?

Challenge

Say aloud daily, "I have the mind of Christ, and I commit to do the Father's will." Learn to take pleasure in putting the needs of others first, and renew your commitment to improve with every challenge.

"And God said, Let us make man in our image, after our likeness . . ."

Genesis 1:26

3

Reflecting the Image of the Anointing

~~~~~~

THE IMAGE YOU PORTRAY QUITE OFTEN DETERMINES how successful you will be in life. Therefore, it is a good idea to take a good look at yourself from time to time to determine how *you* feel about you. The image you have of yourself is important.

I used to be overly concerned about what people thought of me. At times I was extremely uncomfortable with my personal image. But I began to change by listening to my husband's teachings on the anointing and by making a decision to seek the Word of God for answers. I now realize that God's image of me matters most. It's not about establishing an image for myself; instead, it's about conforming to God's image.

For this reason, we must begin to align our thoughts with His. And to reflect His image of the anointing, we must seek God's Word for direction and then make the change.

Our True Value

Too often as Christians, we measure ourselves by the world's perspective and by the things people say. When we do that, we contaminate our minds with garbage that is hard to get rid of. This is how people in the world live—not God's children. The world bases self-value on perception, but our value is based on the Word of God.

Allow me to explain. Imagine a little girl who is not exactly the most beautiful child in the world. If you tell her that she's pretty again and again, several times a day, guess what? She, too, will think she's pretty. She will act pretty and carry herself gracefully. Knowing little girls as well as I do—having three of my own—she'll eventually tell someone else how pretty she is.

But what if that same little girl is told again and again that she is ugly? She'll grow up with a poor self-image. That little girl will, no doubt, feel unworthy, inadequate, or not good enough. These feelings often escalate as we grow older. That's when they have a more damaging effect on our relationships. Feelings of low self-esteem cause undue strain in relationships because we expect someone else to meet a need or fill a void that only God can fill. We may put ourselves in a position to be abused or mistreated because we lack self-worth.

The point is that words create images. The proverb sums it up: "Death and life are in the power of the tongue" (Prov. 18:21 NKJV). Words are powerful, and they shape our destiny. Generally the words spoken to us, whether they are positive or negative, are the same words we remember or speak about ourselves. Jesus declared, "For out of the abundance of the heart the mouth speaketh"

> *If we think positively about ourselves, our words will be positive.*

(Matt. 12:34). In other words, we speak only what is stored in our hearts. If we think positively about ourselves, our words will be positive. On the other hand, if we think negatively about ourselves, our words will be negative. The Bible commands us to guard our hearts (Prov. 4:23), because our self-image is contained there.

If you have been hurt or affected by negative words or if you suffer with low self-esteem for any reason, say this prayer aloud:

Father, in the name of Jesus, I come before You now to submit to You my wounded spirit. Your Word says in 1 Peter 5:7 that I can cast my cares on You because You care for me. In the name of Jesus, I make a decision now to reject all the negative thoughts I have about myself, and I choose to believe only what Your Word says about me. You created me in Your image, and as I become more like Jesus, I am confident, loving, peaceful, and submitted to Your will. According to Acts 20:32, Your Word builds me up; therefore, I renew my mind by reading Your Word daily. I have the mind of Christ. I declare this to be so now in Jesus' name. Amen.

Seeing yourself as a child of God is the best image you can have. The good thing is, you don't have to create an image for yourself because God has already done it for you. From the beginning, God had a specific image in mind for each of us. It was birthed inside Him. In essence, He spoke man out of Himself by using words. Genesis 1:26–27 reads, "And God said, Let us make man in our image, after our likeness . . . So God created man in his own image, in the image of God created he him; male and female created he them." In other words, God said, "Image in Me, be." The entire world and all that is within it was made with God's words. Look through Genesis 1 and you will find these words continuously: "And God said." Every time God created something, He first spoke it into existence. On the sixth day the Bible records, "And God saw every thing that he had made, and, behold, it was very good" (Gen. 1:31).

So words are very important in terms of creating

images inside a person's spirit. What you hear and what you speak determine your level of success or failure. More important, words frame our world. By that I mean words have power—they can either work for or against you. When you speak words, things happen just as they did when God spoke in Genesis 1.

Fervent Prayer

The words you speak must line up with the Word of God. You may be familiar with James 5:16, which says, "The effectual fervent prayer of a righteous man availeth much." This Scripture does not mean that whatever you pray, God will automatically give to you. It means that your prayer will produce favorable results when you include the Word of God.

"So how do I make my prayers effective?" you may ask. You can do it by using Scriptures in your prayer. God will always honor what He says. We read in Isaiah 55:11, "So shall my word be that goeth forth out of my mouth: it shall not return unto me void, but it shall accomplish that which I please, and it shall prosper in the

> *Find the Scriptures that line up with your need, and use them to create an effective prayer.*

thing whereto I sent it." God's Word brings results. It can't fail. The Bible further confirms that everything God says is true (Num. 23:19).

When you talk to God regarding certain issues in your life, find the Scriptures that line up with your need, and use them to create an effective prayer. Here is an example:

Lord, Your Word says in Isaiah 54:17 that no weapon formed against me shall prosper. Cancer is a weapon. Right now I bind the cancer that has formed in my body, and I loose Your healing power. Your Word says in Matthew 16:19 that whatever I bind on earth, You will bind in heaven, and whatever I loose on earth shall be loosed in heaven. I am the healthy protecting my health, and according to Isaiah 53:5, by the stripes of Jesus I am healed. In Jesus' name. Amen.

By saying the Word again and again, you'll become just like the little girl I mentioned earlier. You will not only begin to believe what you say, but you will also have those things you ask: "And if we know that he hear us, whatsoever we ask, we know that we have the petitions that we desired of him" (1 John 5:15).

The same is true of words used in basic conversation. Speak the results you desire rather than wasting time talking about your situation. If you need a raise, don't say, "I need to make more money, but my boss probably won't give me a raise." Guard your words, Child of God, and use them for your benefit just as God did.

The Power of God

God created us in His *image*—His "representation, reflection, likeness, and similarity." The word *image* can also be defined as a "mental picture" or "manifestation." From Romans 8:29, we learn that we are "to be conformed to the image of his Son." Jesus reflects the image of His Father (2 Cor. 4:4), and as we reflect the image of Jesus, we take on the image of His anointing.

> *The anointing is "the burden-removing, yoke-destroying power of God."*

The *anointing* is "the burden-removing, yoke-destroying power of God," as defined in Isaiah 10:27. Jesus, the Anointed One and His Anointing, has the power to get rid of anything that is a burden or yoke in your life. The anointing is an added advantage that allows you to operate in excellence and do away with every distraction in life. You have the ability to tap into that power of anointing, and you must learn to live by it. To live without it is to live without the power God has so graciously given you. Living with it is to operate in the fullness of God's strength rather than your own. It is the place where virtue dwells.

Since you have already been created to look like God, how can you become more like Him in spirit and in character? The answer to this question can be found in 2 Corinthians 3:18: "But we all, with open face beholding as in a glass the glory of the Lord, are changed into the same image from glory to glory, even as by the Spirit of the Lord." When you look into the mirror (the Word of God), you look into God's glory. The more you look into His Word, the more you reflect the image found in His Word, and the transformation takes place.

If this information is a new revelation to you, as it was for me at one time, I pray that you will begin to see yourself the way that God sees you. I am amazed that so many people already know this information yet remain unchanged. Of course, change is never easy. But you must be willing to make the necessary adjustments in order to become better. We could all stand a little improvement here and there. And what better way to begin than by thinking and speaking positive results into your life?

Roadblocks

Several things may become roadblocks as you begin to change your way of thinking where the image of the anointing is concerned:

1. Feelings of Low Self-Image or Lack of Worth

God wants you to consider yourself worthy of His calling. The Bible tells us, "Wherefore also we pray always for you, that our God would count you worthy of this calling, and fulfil all the good pleasure of his goodness, and the work of faith with power: that the name of our Lord Jesus Christ may be glorified in you, and ye in him, according to the grace of our God and the Lord Jesus Christ" (2 Thess. 1:11–12). God created you to fulfill His pleasure: "For I know the thoughts that I think toward you, saith the LORD, thoughts of peace, and not of evil, to give you an expected end" (Jer. 29:11). But the only way to receive God's blessings is to count yourself worthy and to realize that you have been predestined and justified by God from the very beginning of your existence: "For whom he did foreknow, he also did predestinate to be conformed to the image of his Son, that he might be the firstborn among many brethren. Moreover whom he did predestinate, them he also called: and whom he called, them he also justified: and whom he justified, them he also glorified" (Rom. 8:29–30).

Child of God, you must get rid of any old feelings that contradict God's image of you. Instead, lay hold of the truth found in His Word. Perhaps you've been looking for fulfillment in all the wrong places—in people, material things, even drugs or alcohol. Your heavenly Father knows what you need, and only He can provide the things that will last. God wants the best for you. Receive it.

2. Unwillingness to Change the Way You Speak

There is a price to pay in order to live and operate in God's anointing, and it begins with the words you speak. I began to better understand this reality during one of the faith conventions at the church my husband and I pastor, World Changers Church International. Immediately, I had to repent for several things that I had said in the past.

One thing that I recall concerned my daughter Jordan. Sometimes she can say and do the craziest things. I usually responded, "Girl, you act like you've lost your mind." I knew the child hadn't lost her mind, yet I was speaking negative rather than positive things over her life. Proverbs 18:21 warns, "Death and life are in the power of the tongue: and they that love it shall eat the fruit thereof." Another verse that comes to mind can be found in Psalm 141, "Set a watch, O LORD, before my mouth; keep the door of my lips" (v. 3). I didn't want my child to lose her mind! So I had to learn how to set a guard over my mouth. Before the revelation hit me, I

> *And because words have power, you have to be cautious of what you allow to come out of your mouth.*

thought that I could get away with saying whatever I wanted. Now I know better.

We may say things out of habit, or they may be the "in" things to say, such as, "I died laughing," "You ain't ever gonna amount to nothin'," or "I'm broke." Words have power. And because words have power, you have to be cautious of what you allow to come out of your mouth.

3. Stress Over What People May Say

There comes a point in our Christian walk when we have to put the thoughts of others aside, particularly when their thoughts are contrary to God's thoughts. Being in bondage to people will hinder you from obtaining the things God has in store for you. I wouldn't be where I am today if I were still in bondage to people. As followers of Christ, we have the goal of pleasing God, not man. Paul spoke to this issue: "For do I now persuade men, or God? or do I seek to please men? for if I yet pleased men, I should not be the servant of Christ" (Gal. 1:10).

Many times we want to be servants of the Lord without paying the price for change. A servant does what the master tells him to do. He doesn't run off and do what he wants to do. When the servant chooses to disobey, he puts himself in a position to become a hindrance or burden to the master.

Being a good servant requires obedience. If you are not willing to put God first, you disrespect Him and His calling on your life. You can't serve God by being in bondage to people, so don't be ashamed to conform to God's way.

4. A Preference to Maintain a Worldly Image

God wants His image to be evident in our lives. When we choose to reflect other images, such as the ones we see in the world, we cross over into idolatry because we value those images above God. We have to make sure that we don't create other images contrary to God's Word. God says He will spoil the images of those whose hearts are divided (Hos. 10:1–2).

Concentrate on building the image reflected in God's Word. When thoughts creep into your mind that don't line up with the Word, pull down that stronghold. Use your mouth to stop the attack of the enemy: "Casting down imaginations, and every high thing that exalteth itself against the knowledge of God, and bringing into captivity every thought to the obedience of Christ" (2 Cor. 10:5).

> *I walk in the image of the anointing.*

Don't allow the devil to tempt you by making the grass on the other side of the fence appear greener. God's way is best (Ps. 18:30).

Learning how to establish the image of the anointing isn't difficult, Child of God. The directions are right there in the instruction manual—God's Word. Begin now to confess the Word over your life daily. Make confessions a part of your prayer time. Say them aloud several times a day until you see the manifestation. Finally, always do what the Word of God says to do.

> But be ye doers of the word, and not hearers only, deceiving your own selves. For if any be a hearer of the word, and not a doer, he is like unto a man beholding his natural face in a glass . . . But whoso looketh into the perfect law of liberty, and continueth therein, he being not a forgetful hearer, but a doer of the work, this man shall be blessed in his deed. (James 1:22–23, 25)

Confession

I walk in the image of the anointing. I guard my tongue and speak only what is good. Through my words, I shape my world. I make a decision now to begin using the Word of God in every prayer, and I believe that I have everything I ask according to Your will. I declare this to be so now in Jesus' name. Amen.

Study Questions

1. Take a long look in the mirror. What image do you see physically, spiritually, and emotionally?

2. In what ways does the image you have of yourself match the image God has of you? In what ways does it not?

3. What roles do positive and negative words play in the image you see?

4. Whose approval do you seek?

5. Do you allow your self-worth to be determined by your own opinion, the opinion of others, or God's opinion?

6. How much time are you willing to invest in God's Word in order to become the person He has called you to be?

7. On a typical day, do you say more negative or positive things about yourself, your situation, and others?

8. Are you willing to research the Scriptures that relate to the issues in your life and take the time to speak them over your circumstances? Or are you more apt to grumble and complain about those issues?

Challenge

Make a conscious decision to spend more time with God each day. The more time you spend with Him, the more you will become like Him, and the clearer you will hear His voice.

"Submit yourselves therefore to God"

James 4:7

4

The Key to Releasing
the Anointing

LEARNING TO BE SUBMISSIVE HAS PERHAPS BEEN THE MOST valuable lesson in my life. For years I hated the word, let alone the thought of being submissive to anyone. I used to think God had something against women. It just didn't seem right to me that women should be treated so unfairly. It was not until I learned the true meaning of submission that I understood its value and rewards. And indeed there are great rewards.

Submission has been taught incorrectly for many years. In many cases, there has been a lack of balance in the instruction. My objective is not only to clarify the meaning of submission, but also to demonstrate how

Satan has caused many of us to think of submission as a negative thing. With that in mind, I want you to approach the subject as if you've never learned anything about submission before. Erase all that garbage about it being a form of slavery, inferiority, or stupidity. Submission doesn't mean that you are insignificant. That's a trick of the devil. So hang in there. The revelation you're about to tap into will take you to another level in God, and you will be blessed beyond measure.

The True Meaning of Submission

The word *submission* means "to yield or surrender to authority." It can be applied to a particular person, such as your boss, spouse, or pastor. Another definition for *submission* is "to comply with the commands of a superior." This means to abide by set rules, standards of procedure, or commandments. *Submission* also means "obedience." And that's the word I ran from for a long time.

I could not see myself obeying anyone, especially my husband. He has told the story time after time of how I searched to no end look-ing for a definition of *submission* other than "obedience." I was deter-mined to find another

> *Submission is first and foremost unto God.*

meaning. I was not going to be made to feel inferior to him. No way!

Submission to God

Then I learned a valuable lesson about submission: Submission is first and foremost *unto* God. The word broken into two parts, *sub* and *mission*, means "to get under the mission of another." It's what Jesus' whole life was about—submitting to the will of the Father. If He could do it, we can too. After all, we're not being asked to do more than Jesus did.

I recognized that God wasn't being unfair when He established submission. He created it for our benefit. Too often we regard submission as a means of losing our identity, especially those who are married. For a long time, I was afraid of losing my identity in marriage. But I had to realize that my identity is based solely on the Word of God, and so is my submission. Jesus provided for us the perfect example. He "made himself of no reputation, and took upon him the form of a servant . . . And being found in fashion as a man, he humbled himself, and became obedient unto death, even the death of the cross" (Phil. 2:7–8).

We should never try to establish an identity apart from the Word. That puts us in an area where we are unable to submit to God. To be honest, we're in rebellion when we live contrary to the Word.

It's for Everyone

Submission is for everyone. Here are two verses that support this fact. James 4:7 commands us to "submit [ourselves] therefore to God." And 1 Peter 5:5 urges, "Likewise, ye younger, submit yourselves unto the elder. Yea, all of you be subject one to another, and be clothed with humility: for God resisteth the proud, and giveth grace to the humble." Notice that there is no gender attached to these verses. I don't know who came up with the idea that submission is only for women. I repeat, submission is for everyone.

As submission relates to marriage, Ephesians 5:21 says, "Submitting yourselves one to another in the fear of God." However, verse 22 has often been the focus of many teachings: "Wives, submit yourselves unto your own husbands, as unto the Lord." The emphasis on this Scripture explains how much of the balance has been lost. Many teachings have highlighted this verse without comment on the preceding verse.

But it is true that wives are commanded by God to submit to their husbands. Read these verses and you'll see why:

For the husband is the head of the wife, even as Christ is the head of the church: and he is the saviour of the body. Therefore as the church is subject unto Christ, so let the wives be to their own husbands in every thing. Husbands, love your wives, even as Christ also loved the church, and gave himself for it; that he might sanctify and cleanse it with the washing of water by the word . . . So ought men to love their wives as their own bodies. He that loveth his wife loveth himself. For no man ever yet hated his own flesh; but nourisheth and cherisheth it, even as the Lord the church. (Eph. 5:23–29)

Wives should submit to their husbands for several reasons. The husband is appointed by God to be the *head*, "authority or responsible party," over the wife. In essence, the husband is to love, protect, provide for, nourish, and cherish his wife. His job is also to sanctify and cleanse his bride by following Christ's example and by providing leadership and support through the Word of God. The husband's job is to take care of his wife. Then she is enhanced and becomes a complement to him: a holy and virtuous woman of whom he can be proud.

> *Ephesians 5:21 requires that each partner submit to the other.*

Again, realize that you are not the only one who is expected to submit. Ephesians 5:21 requires that each partner submit to the other. Your husband should also submit himself to you. His response to you should show a spirit of willingness to support and assist without apprehension. I remember when Creflo would ask me for a glass of water every night without fail. He'd already be in bed, and I'd be preparing to get in bed. Just as I'd pull the covers back to crawl in, he'd say, "Honey, can you get me a glass of water?" No matter how tired I was, I'd agree and bring him the water. One night, the tables turned. He'd had a long day and was desperately trying to get into bed. I'd already settled in. For some strange reason, I suddenly became thirsty. This time, I asked *him* for a glass of water. I could tell that he was tempted to complain and ask me to get my own water. Instead, he brought me the water and jokingly said, "Do you want a pizza with that?" Later, he told me that he had never realized his pattern to always ask me for a glass of water at the last minute. Neither had he realized the extent of my submissiveness to him. He admitted it was a true lesson in submission that humbled him greatly.

You see, balance is the key here. And as long as everyone is going out of the way to serve and respect the other, there is peace. It makes you feel good about each other and your relationship when you can count on your mate to be there and to submit willingly.

Husbands are also required by God to live a certain way with their wives to ensure that their prayers are answered: "Likewise, ye husbands, dwell with them according to knowledge, giving honour unto the wife . . . that your prayers be not hindered" (1 Peter 3:7). Your husband has to dwell in knowledge with you. He should take the time to learn who you are and how to live with you in harmony. He should also seek knowledge and wisdom from God as he learns to serve you and accept you for who you are. If he doesn't, and the two of you are living in strife, God says that your husband's prayers will not be answered. It's useless to pray until the two of you get it right. Living in strife can hinder the anointing in your marriage and in your lives individually.

Finally, God commands husbands to honor their wives. You should be a priority to your husband, considered first after God. The word *honor* means "to give authority of yourself over to another person." He gives you the authority to speak into his life and to be obeyed.

There are truly great benefits when we live by the Word. Most women like to be pampered and treated with care. And we certainly appreciate men who are supportive and provide for us. These things come without much effort from men whose wives willingly and diligently submit to them. God intended it to be that way. His plan is so much better than our own. I can tell you from experience that there's nothing like it.

If you take on the spirit of Christ and submit to your husband, support his mission, listen to his plans, and nurture his vision, there is no telling what he'll do for you. He will begin doing things you didn't even ask him to do. I'm telling you, the benefits are awesome! Honey, your relationship will begin to bear witness to the kind of fruit or blessings God promises that we will have when we obey Him. And romance will be the icing on the cake. Hallelujah!

You see, your submission is as unto God; you act as if you are submitting directly to God. Despite what your husband does or doesn't do, you line up with the Word, and God will honor your obedience. Remember, submit to God first. In that way, as you serve your husband, you serve God, and both are pleased.

If you decide not to be submissive to your husband's authority, you forfeit your opportunity to claim the benefits package. Not only that, you remove yourself from the umbrella of God's protection. Submission is for your protection. When you make a decision to move out of the will of God, you move into dangerous territory—deception, influence, and confusion, just to name a few. Don't try to justify your position by complaining that your husband is not doing his part.

> *Submission is for your protection.*

It's Not About Your Feelings

Submission has nothing to do with your feelings. It's not about whether you want to submit. You do it because God says so. Your obedience can bring about a dynamic change in your relationship with your spouse and with God. "Well, Sister Taffi, what if he hurts my feelings? And what about those days when he doesn't act like a man of God?" you may ask. Stay the same. Don't return evil with evil.

The Word says, "Likewise, ye wives, be in subjection to your own husbands; that, if any obey not the word, they also may without the word be won by the conversation of the wives" (1 Peter 3:1). In essence, your obedience to God influences your husband in areas where he lacks obedience to God. This also applies to a woman with an unsaved spouse. The Word says your lifestyle and conversation are capable of getting him born again. So just suck it up, Honey, and keep right on serving him. He'll change. God will see to it. (You may want to use 1 Peter 3:1 as part of your confession when you are tempted to do otherwise.)

When God made woman, He made her to be man's help *meet*, or "one who is suitable, adaptable, or fit" (Gen. 2:18). *Help* is defined as "one who provides aid or assistance." During Adam's time, there was no other living creature qualified to be his help. Therefore, God created woman especially for man. Isn't that something? All this time you thought you were made independently of man, but in reality you were made exclusively *for* him (1 Cor. 7:34). Eve didn't have her own identity per se because she was part of Adam. She not only complemented him; she completed him as well.

When a woman is saved and her spouse is not, she may neglect her position as his help because she doesn't see him walking uprightly. She becomes discouraged, and at times she loses hope in his ability to change. Unfortunately, her reluctance to be a faithful helper results in his failure to answer the call on his life and thus the call on their lives as a couple. She then becomes part of the problem rather than the solution. If you're in this position, I encourage you to renew your commitment to do God's will and immediately begin to serve your husband as his help. Don't condemn yourself because there is no condemnation in Christ (Rom. 8:1). Simply make the change and move on.

There are things you can do to win your man over to God without being pushy. We talked about the opportunity for change earlier. When he witnesses your submission and pleasant conversation, your husband's disposition will begin to change and take on the character of Christ (1 Peter 3:1). However, you can also apply faith pressure in your prayers and confessions. Find Scriptures that support your situation. For example, 1 Peter 3:8 talks about being "of one mind." Don't put more confidence in your situation than in God's Word by making negative comments, such as, "He'll never change." The Word of

God is true. Stand on it, and don't compromise your position with God by failing to remember your husband in your prayers. Place total confidence in God.

So often we fail to realize how paramount our relationships really are. In the beginning God created a woman to be a part of her husband. Even though we're living in a different era, God's plan for us has not changed. And to be honest, I see a whole lot of men around here who need help, and they're married. Oops! Did I step on your toes?

Help that man, Honey! Be the virtuous woman God has called you to be. "Do him good and not evil all the days of [your] life" (Prov. 31:12). Dress him up. Submit to his plans. Help him out a little. If you could see some of those old pictures of Creflo, you'd say, "Thank God for Sister Taffi." On the other hand, if you saw some of my old pictures, you'd say, "Hallelujah for Creflo." But it's all good, praise God! We're good for each other.

I like to use this acronym for help: humble, efficient, loving, playmate. Of course, this applies only to married women. If you aren't married, we'll have to figure out something different for you. Perhaps this one will work: humble, efficient, loving, person. You have no business being someone's playmate. Honey, if he hasn't put a ring on your finger and lawfully married you under God's holy ordinance, forget about it.

Now enough about marriage and submission. If you're single, you're probably cheering at this point. But let me encourage you by paraphrasing something that my husband once said at a family convention. Often, we want to hear or read information that is specifically for us. For example, if you're single, you want information that is relative to being single. The same is true if you're married. There's nothing wrong with that. However, the Bible applies to everyone; just follow the instructions. If I gave you a recipe to bake a chocolate cake, it would come out the same whether you were married or single. In other words, follow the recipe. Now, let's discover how to release the anointing.

> *The Bible applies to everyone; just follow the instructions.*

It Involves Faith

Submission must be done in faith. The Bible says anything other than faith is sin (Rom. 14:23). *Faith* is "believing and acting on what we believe." In order to release the burden-removing, yoke-destroying power of God (Isa. 10:27), faith must accompany submission. If we go through the motions of submission with a bad attitude, our submission is not unto the Lord: "But without faith it is impossible to please Him" (Heb. 11:6 NKJV). I think this passage says it best:

Servants, obey in all things your masters according to the flesh; not with eyeservice, as menpleasers; but in singleness of heart, fearing God: and whatsoever ye do, do it heartily, as to the Lord, and not unto men; knowing that of the Lord ye shall receive the reward of the inheritance: for ye serve the Lord Christ. (Col. 3:22–24)

Whether you are submitting to your boss, husband, or pastor, you must do it with faith. Otherwise, you disqualify yourself from receiving God's reward. I don't know about you, but I like rewards—especially those given by God.

You cannot entertain fear and doubt. You must learn to trust God. Your mind may say, *Child, forget that submission business. You may wind up getting hurt or used.* But the Word has a solution for thoughts that challenge God's promises: "Casting down imaginations, and every high thing that exalteth itself against the knowledge of God, and bringing into captivity every thought to the obedience of Christ" (2 Cor. 10:5). And James clearly stated, "Submit yourselves therefore to God. Resist the devil, and he will flee from you" (James 4:7).

The devil doesn't want you to have any peace. He doesn't want you to prosper in your life or relationships. And the only way you can have either is to submit to God's will. That's why Satan makes submission seem like such a bad thing. Satan will do anything he can to keep you out of the will of God.

Even if submission is the only area you're lacking in your Christian walk, that level of disobedience gives him a foothold. And you don't want that. The devil can and will wreak havoc in your life in ways you can't imagine: Not just in your relationships, but in your job, at church, even in your mental well-being. Don't allow him to do it, child of God. Take authority over the devil right now, in Jesus' name!

Here is the formula for releasing the anointing in your life:

SUBMISSION + FAITH = ANOINTING

Don't go around thinking you're doing someone else a favor when you submit. You're doing yourself a favor. Your obedience, coupled with faith, will cause God to open up the floodgates of anointing in your life. The anointing is the burden-removing, yoke-destroying power of God that produces the ability to do the uncommon in your life. It's God's superability on your natural ability that gets supernatural results. I don't know about you, but I need that kind of power in my life, especially in these last days.

Therefore, submit yourself to God first, then submit to authority in every area of your life. You will not only please God, but you, too, will be pleased with God's response to your obedience.

Confession

I submit my entire being to You, Father, in faith. And I thank You for the authority You have placed over my life. As I submit to those in authority over me, help me to be mindful that submission is for my protection. I repent for areas in my life where I have not been willing to submit. Your Word says that when I repent, You are faithful and just to forgive me and to cleanse me of all unrighteousness (1 John 1:9). I will operate neither dishonorably nor rebelliously because it will hinder You and Your anointing from intervening on my behalf. I receive now the release of Your anointing to do, with excellence, all that You desire. I declare this to be so now in Jesus' name. Amen.

Study Questions

1. On a scale of 1 to 10, 10 being the highest, where do you rank in the area of submission to God, your spouse, pastor, parents, or employer?

2. In which areas have you allowed rebellion to intervene?

3. How willing are you to submit to those in authority over you—such as your pastor, spouse, boss, or parent(s)?

4. What evidence is there in your life that proves you are totally submitted to God?

5. In what order do you seek direction to handle life's problems and challenges: your friends, family, spouse, self, or God?

6. How will a submissive attitude impact your rate of success in overcoming daily challenges?

7. When faced with challenges, do you respond with faith, or do you react with fear and worry?

Challenge

Evaluate your level of submission in every area in life, and be willing to make changes where needed. Keep in mind that submission is for your protection, and it is the key to releasing the anointing in your life.

Because they have no changes, therefore they fear not God.

—Psalm 55:19

5

The Anointing to Change

~~~~

A COMMITMENT TO PLEASE GOD REQUIRES AN EQUALLY
important commitment to change. The two go together.
While you are reading this book, I believe the Spirit is
revealing to you areas in your life that need improvement. However, in order to change, we must understand
what change is and begin to apply the things we learn.
The definition of *change* is threefold. First, it means "to
make different," second, it means "to take an alternative
course or direction," and third, it means "to undergo a
process, transition, and substitution." Making a decision
to change is making a decision to take a course that dif-
fers from the norm.

Change is a continual, unfolding process. Rarely does it happen overnight. And since learning is also a continuous process, every born-again believer should make change a way of life. The Amplified Bible says it this way:

> Do not be conformed to this world (this age), [fashioned after and adapted to its external, superficial customs], but be transformed (changed) by the [entire] renewal of your mind [by its new ideals and its new attitude], so that you may prove [for yourselves] what is the good and acceptable and perfect will of God, even the thing which is good and acceptable and perfect [in His sight for you]. (Rom. 12:2)

The transformation that God desires for us is a complete renewal of the mind. It is the initial process by which change takes place. The word *transformation* means "metamorphosis or change of condition or form." For example, metamorphosis occurs in the life of a caterpillar when it transforms into a butterfly.

The process of salvation is quite similar. When we make a decision to become born again, we make a conscious decision to turn away from the sinful nature that has dominated our lives and instead become new creatures in Christ. In other words, we change our condition of living. The Bible states, "Therefore if any man be in

Christ, he is a new creature: old things are passed away; behold, all things are become new" (2 Cor. 5:17).

This Scripture confirms that once we accept Jesus as our Lord and Savior, we are no longer the same. We become new persons who have never before existed. I'm so glad God didn't just fix us up and slap a bandage on us; instead, He made us brand new. Glory to God! That fact alone should be enough to make us want to change immediately. Your attitude should be, "Look out, world, here I come!"

Newness Just for You

God wants to do something new with and through you. And as you begin to spend more time in His presence, praying in the Holy Spirit, you'll begin to experience the newness God has predestined just for you. You'll begin to live at a newer and better level. Child of God, He loves you so much. He wants to see you change, and He is committed to help you through. He is not trying to force you into anything or take anything away. He has so many great things in store for you; however, you will never experience them without change.

Again, change is a process. God never intended for you to have the born-again experience and just stop living, learning, and maturing. He wants your life to be a continuous process of transformation that begins with salvation and ultimately extends to other areas. For instance, God wants you to become renewed in your way of thinking regarding health. The same is true of wealth, prosperity, and deliverance. Honey, He wants you to believe that you can be delivered from sickness, disease, lack, and every other form of bondage. God wants you to lay hold of an entire new way of living!

When our minds are renewed, we see things differently, more ideally, and with a new attitude. God promises us that by making a conscious effort to renew the mind, we will be able to prove His perfect will for us. Child of God, He wants to demonstrate, through you, the proof and goodness of being in His perfect will.

For the process of change to take place, you must become more disciplined. That means saying no to the flesh—those selfish and carnal desires for relationships, activities, and things that do not line up with the Word of God. For example, a carnal desire could be your urge to curse someone out for getting on your nerves. In addition, sleeping around, drinking, and going to the club are also considered walking in the flesh. Romans 8:1–8 tells us:

> There is therefore now no condemnation to them which are in Christ Jesus, who walk not after the flesh, but after the Spirit. For the law of the Spirit of life in Christ Jesus hath made me free from the law of sin and death. For what the law could not do, in that it was weak through the flesh, God sending his own Son in the

likeness of sinful flesh, and for sin, condemned sin in
the flesh: that the righteousness of the law might be fulfilled in us, who walk not after the flesh, but after the
Spirit. . . . For to be carnally minded is death; but to be
spiritually minded is life and peace. Because the carnal
mind is enmity against God: for it is not subject to the
law of God, neither indeed can be. So then they that
are in the flesh cannot please God.

The last sentence in this passage should be enough to
make us want to change. In essence, it says those who are
not willing to conform to God's standards and guidelines
can never please Him. By choosing to remain in our old
carnal or "worldly" ways, we show an outright disregard
for God and His Word. The carnal mind is *enmity* or an
"enemy" to God (v. 7). It also leads to death (v. 6).

This passage lists several advantages to living according to God's way:

1. There is no condemnation (v. 1).

2. There is freedom from bondage to old habits and
   addictions (v. 2).

3. We have life and peace (v. 6).

I also like the added advantage referenced in verse 14,
which reads, "For as many as are led by the Spirit of God,

73

they are the sons of God." That means we are part of Him—His children.

The born-again experience enables the Spirit of God to come inside you, making your spirit alive to God. The Holy Spirit gives you the opportunity to live without being controlled by your flesh. So it is important to renew your mind so that carnal thoughts and actions won't contain you.

God has given us several agents by which we can change and lay hold of the newness of life God has promised. He has given us His name, His Word, His authority, His Spirit, His power, His wisdom, and every anointing that we need.

But how do we let go of our ways and grab hold of God's? Colossians 3:10 has the answer: "Put on the new man, which is renewed in knowledge after the image of him that created him." We renew our way of thinking—our knowledge—by staying in God's Word. Just as faith comes by hearing the Word of God (Rom. 10:17), so does renewal of the mind. Titus 3:5 says that the Word of God washes us, cleanses us, and gives us a new birth, a renewing by the Holy Spirit. By seeking God's Word for direction on how we should live, we make the Word the final authority in our lives. In other words, whatever the Bible says, goes.

One way to begin the process of change is to replace old habits with new ones. Substitution is an appropriate way to approach change. For example, the best way to help your child change his behavior is to offer him a substitute to replace the thing being taken away. If your son likes listening to secular rap music, but you're opposed to foul language or negative images, find a Christian rap artist who uses the Word of God in music lyrics and whose music is appealing to your child.

Similarly, if you lose your temper often, begin to substitute that energy with a gentle word and surprise those around you by remaining silent before responding. By doing so, you will allow yourself time to think clearly before you speak, and most often you will avoid saying and doing things that you may later regret (James 1:19).

The same is true of relationships. How many times have you heard someone say, "Don't tell me how much you love me; show me?" If your spouse expresses a desire for you to change in certain areas of your life, you should be willing to make the necessary adjustments. God says, "If ye love me, keep my commandments" (John 14:15). In essence He is saying, "If you love Me, show Me your willingness to change."

Love is often expressed through change. If you're in a relationship where there is a resistance to change, it's not love because love gives. As my husband, Creflo, once said, "No love, no change. No change, no love." I remember counseling battered women for whom this rule applies. Many times their husbands would abuse them, then apologize by saying, "I love you and I'm willing to change." However, after deciding to try again, some wives would go back and before long experience the same things. Come on, now. That's not love. Love only wants what is good and beneficial for the other, which is God's desire for us as we relate to Him. He wants us to be willing to make the necessary changes to improve our relationship with Him and our lives overall.

Whether it is marriage, friendship, or family relationships, oftentimes there is a desire to see the other person change. But if you want to *see* change, you must be willing to *sow* change. In every relationship, there is room for improvement. If you want the other person to change, you must be willing to take the first step. Do your part by seeking God's Word for answers regarding your concerns, and make confessions regarding the issues that need resolution. Be willing to pray until you see the manifestation of God's intervention. And demonstrate your willingness to make adjustments in your life. It's easy to sit back and complain; the biggest challenge is accepting the reality that you, too, need to change.

Barriers to Change

The two most common barriers to change are pride and fear. *Pride* is "an exaggerated opinion of yourself." It's thinking you're something when you're not. Satan is the originator of pride. Isaiah 14:12–14 and Ezekiel 28:14–18 reveal the cause of Satan's fall. He thought more highly of himself than he should (Rom. 12:3). Because he was beautiful and desired the same honor and respect as God, he lost his God-appointed position as an archangel. In clearer terms, pride moved him out of the will of God. And Satan will use pride to get you out of God's will—a position you cannot afford.

Fear is designed to keep you in bondage. If Satan can prevent you from stepping out in faith and make you skeptical of living according to God's Word, he will have dominion in your life and will hinder change and spiritual maturity.

Pride and fear work together. Satan uses these tools to torment you and keep you in a place of containment. He wants you to believe that there is a limit to what you can achieve. Rather than believing God for complete restoration of health, Satan wants you to believe that you can be healed only of a few symptoms. He wants you to believe that there is a glass ceiling to your promotion and increase. But the fact of the matter is, there are no limits where God is concerned. Nothing is impossible for Him (Matt. 19:26; Mark 10:27; Luke 1:37).

From Glory to Glory

Now, I'd be going overboard if I told you or implied that change is easy. I'll be the first to say that it is not. Change is often difficult because the flesh has a natural tendency to resist. Many people want change, but they are not willing to do what it takes to achieve the desired result. Losing weight is a good example. Hundreds of thousands of people in this country want to change their physical appearance. But when it comes to exercising discipline by changing what they eat, when they eat, and how much they eat, they're not willing to make the sacrifice.

Here are four ways to respond appropriately to change:

1. *Listen carefully* (James 1:19). Be open to the idea of change. Allow the other person an opportunity to completely present his thoughts.

2. *Before you respond, judge yourself* (1 Cor. 11:31–32). If you judge yourself, according to the written Word of God, you will not be judged. If you fail to judge yourself, certain areas in your life will go unchanged.

3. *Don't react; instead, take the time to respond* (Prov. 18:13). Don't blow things out of proportion! Listen carefully and respond accordingly.

4. *Beware of offense* (Matt. 11:6; Luke 7:23). When you are offended, or feel the need to defend or justify yourself, you fail to see the truth of the matter.

The Amplified Bible reads in 2 Corinthians 3:18, "All of us, as with unveiled face, [because we] continued to behold [in the Word of God] as in a mirror the glory of the Lord, are constantly being transfigured into His very own image in ever increasing splendor and from one degree of glory to another; [for this comes] from the Lord [Who is] the Spirit." It is by the Spirit of the Lord that change progresses from glory to glory. By looking in the mirror—God's Word—we are better able to identify the areas where change is needed. It is also through the Spirit of God that we are able to tap in to the anointing for change. The more time we spend in the Word, the more we will be transformed into the likeness of our heavenly Father. Jesus is the expressed image of the Father. And in this way we become more like Him.

The good thing is, we don't have to make ourselves into His image. The Word is designed to do it for us. Therefore, we must apply faith pressure on God's Word to receive the manifestation of change. Our part is to know the Word and obey the Spirit. God's part is to make sure the transformation takes place when we do so.

No matter how we see change or how we feel about it, God has designed it for our benefit. After all, our ways are not His ways (Isa. 55:8). God sees change as an opportunity for us to expand, grow, mature, and develop. It is His way of enlarging His presence in our lives. It is also His way of promoting us from one level to the next.

Steps Toward Change

Now that we've established the foundation and barriers of change, I want to share with you seven important steps toward making change a way of life.

1. Make a quality decision to change.

2. Be open to correction and be teachable.

3. Turn your will over to God completely.

4. Begin to see God's Word as a mirror for change.

5. Guard your heart by controlling the things you hear, see, and speak.

6. Control your thoughts.

7. Avoid negative exposure through people, places, and activities.

To transform and maintain areas in your life that need change, you must avoid Satan's attempts to trick you. The Bible admonishes us in 1 Thessalonians 5:22 to avoid the very appearance of evil. In other words, at all cost, avoid those things, people, and situations that get you off track. For example, if you used drugs in the past, avoid your old hangout and old friends who have not decided to change. Or if you're trying to become healthier and lose weight, stop going to the all-you-can-eat food bar. Abstain from the things that appeal to your flesh (1 Peter 2:11). Instead, tap into the power of God's anointing. Say along with Paul, "I can do all things through Christ which strengtheneth me" (Phil. 4:13).

There is an anointing available for change. I encourage you to make a list of the areas in your life that need change. Follow the steps provided, make the daily confessions that pertain to change, and ask God for assistance. Remember, you can do nothing in and of yourself, but all things are made possible with God (Matt. 19:26; Mark 10:27).

Confession

Father, in the name of Jesus, give me the anointing to change. I yield myself to Your presence and Your power. I open my heart, my eyes, my ears, and my spirit to hear from You. Show me the areas in my life that need change. I now realize that it is Your desire that I change, so that You may prove your good, perfect, and acceptable will for my life (Rom. 12:2). I thank You now, Lord, for the beautiful new creation You will make of me. I declare this so now, in Jesus' name. Amen.

Study Questions

1. Think of three areas in your life that need change. How will you go about making the necessary adjustments?

2. According to John 14:15, if we love God, we keep His commandments. How does your Christian walk reflect your love for the Father?

3. What can you do to get someone else—your spouse, friend, child, or relative—to change certain things in his life?

4. What are the two most common barriers to change? What is preventing you from changing?

5. How does Satan try to interfere in your process of transformation? What can you do to stop him?

6. Why does God want us to change? According to the Word, what are some of the benefits that result from it?

7. Based on your past experiences, are you easily offended when someone points out an area in your life that needs changing? If so, how do you generally react, and what can you do to prevent this from happening again in the future?

Challenge

Make a list of three to five areas in your life that need changing. Take a few minutes to look up Scriptures that reflect the changes you want to make and memorize them. When the temptation to give in to your flesh arises, quote what you have memorized. Keep a thirty-day journal of your progress. You'll be surprised at the difference this will make in your life.

To every thing there is a season, and a time to every purpose under the heaven . . . He hath made every thing beautiful in his time.

—Ecclesiastes 3:1, 11

6

Purpose in the Journey

~~~~

GOD HAS A PURPOSE FOR EVERYTHING THAT HE DOES, AND He had a purpose when He created you. Many women ask themselves, What is God's purpose for my life? The answer can be found by reading the Word of God and by spending quality time with Him. The more time you spend with God, the more familiar His voice and His personality will become. Discovering God's purpose for your life is the most rewarding and fulfilling experience that any child of God can achieve. For a virtuous woman, it should be the motivation that prompts you to begin each day and the encouragement to go on in difficult times. Personally, I want to accomplish God's entire purpose for my life.

God's Will for You

You are God's daughter. And, as in most parent-child relationships, there is a natural tendency to want to please Him. If you have never considered fulfilling the will of God for your life, I encourage you to begin seeking God for His will by asking Him directly, "What is Your purpose for my life? And where do I begin?"

In Proverbs 19:21, we read, "There are many devices in a man's heart; nevertheless the counsel of the LORD, that shall stand." The word *devices* in this verse refers to "plans or desires." You may have many plans and desires in your heart, but do all of them line up with God's plans and desires? Many times we establish goals and ideas that differ from God's. However, we must understand and submit to God's purpose for our lives in order to carry out His will for us on this earth.

One of the things that I planned to do after I finished college was to work as an administrator in a mental health hospital. I had always wanted to do that. But when I met Creflo, everything changed. I later realized that God had a different plan for my life.

Don't get me wrong, God doesn't take pleasure in interrupting your plans. However, He does take pleasure in your submission to His plans for your life. What I planned for my life was totally different from what God planned. I never thought that I would be working full-time in the ministry or would be married to a minister. The last thing I wanted to do was to marry a preacher. But God knew what was best for me. He knew what I could handle. I just praise God that I had enough sense to submit to His will.

If you are married, part of the will of God for your life includes being a help to your husband. In Genesis 2:18, the Lord said, "It is not good that the man should be alone; I will make him an help meet for him." First of all, God said that it was not *good*—lovely, delightful, comfortable, right, pleasant, excellent, joyful, or well— for man to be alone. As a solution, God made woman. Just as the Holy Spirit helps you, God has called you to help your husband. You are expected to help him carry out the purpose that God has created him to fulfill. As a result, you fulfill the plan God has for your lives as a couple (Prov. 18:22).

I now realize that I was created to be Creflo's help. As his help, I bring him a state of living that is lovely, delightful, and comfortable. I want you to realize how serious and sacred the holy calling of marriage is. God "hath saved us, and called us with an holy calling, not according to our works, but according to his own purpose and grace, which was given us in Christ Jesus before the world began" (2 Tim. 1:9). Part of this holy calling is the ministry of helps. Never take your role as a helpmeet casually; neither take it for granted. Instead, see it as a holy, precious, sacred, and very important position in God's sight.

The Bible tells us that "there is difference also between a wife and a virgin. The unmarried woman careth for the things of the Lord, that she may be holy both in body and in spirit: but she that is married careth for the things of the world, how she may please her husband" (1 Cor. 7:34). God has a different, yet very significant responsibility for single women. First of all, He expects the unmarried to remain pure and holy—a virgin in body and in spirit. And second, He expects her to submit wholly and completely to Him. If you are single, rejoice in the Lord! The will of God for your life is to exclusively tend to His work. You should regard this as a coveted season in life of undistracted devotion to God. Praise God!

However, if you are married, your concern should be to please and help your husband. Being concerned about the things of the world does not mean that you become disconnected from God. On the contrary, once a woman marries and begins to have children, she should seek the Lord more than ever regarding His will for her life as a good wife and mother. She takes on the awesome tasks of helping her man of God carry out God's will for his life and training the precious children entrusted to her by God.

Ways to Help

I know that God holds me responsible for the task of being Creflo's help. With this in mind, I refuse to do anything that would hinder the successful completion of this assignment. I take seriously this proverb: "Whoso findeth a wife findeth a good thing, and obtaineth favour of the LORD" (Prov. 18:22). As my husband teaches, the "thing" in this Scripture refers to marriage, not the wife. And it should be good. If you haven't already, I encourage you to decide in your heart that you will make your marriage a "good thing." Purpose to be good help, not nagging, unproductive, or annoying help.

To be good help, you should frequently ask your husband how you can be a good help to him. Let's say I call my friend Lisa and say, "Lisa, I want you to help me move." If she agrees to help me, but comes over and starts boxing things without asking me what I *need* her to do, she is not really helping me. Asking is the best way to ensure your success. Turn to your husband and say, "Honey, what can I do to help you?" You need to ask him this question not only when he is running around the house before an important meeting but also ask him consistently as part of your daily communication. You are more likely to please him this way.

After you find out how you can help your husband, *be willing to do what he says!* If he tells you that he would like

> *You can also help your husband by motivating him to become the man God has called him to be.*

you to talk less and listen more, do it. Don't get an attitude and say, "You need to do the same thing," or "You should be glad that I don't talk as much as I used to." Just do as he says. Do your best to make life for him pleasant, enjoyable, and comfortable.

You can also help your husband by motivating him to become the man God has called him to be. You may not like several characteristics or habits of your husband. However, instead of nagging him, declare to God and to yourself that you will help him become better in those areas. For example, my husband once had a challenge with eating sweets. We both realized that this habit wasn't the best for his health. So instead of condemning him or making him feel bad about it, I encouraged him to eat better foods. I decided to alter some of my poor eating habits, and together we made the necessary changes to become healthier. Through the conviction of the Holy Spirit and my decision to get involved and help him, we have overcome challenges in this area, and as a result we have become healthier.

A third way to help your husband is to represent him in an honorable manner: "For a man indeed ought not to cover his head, forasmuch as he is the image and glory of God: but the woman is the glory of the man" (1 Cor. 11:7). Let's examine the last part of that verse, "The woman is the glory of the man." *Glory* means "expressed image or representative." It also means "the outward appearance which comes from within and reflects splendor and brightness." In other words, you represent your husband. The splendor and anointing that show on your countenance—in your words and actions—represent your husband. If you're single, you are the expressed image of Jesus, and you should concentrate on making Him look good.

I hope that when people see me, they see my husband because we are one. Together, Creflo and I are the image of Jesus. We desire to truthfully represent Him in all that we do. Our prayer is that people see Jesus in us and in all that we do. Ask yourself these questions: What image am I expressing? Am I one with my husband? Do I represent him well? If you are single, these questions apply to your reflected image of Jesus.

Jesus was the expressed image of His Father, "the brightness of his [God's] glory, and the express image of his person" (Heb. 1:3). He always spoke of carrying out His Father's plan, and He spoke only those things that His Father approved of or directed Him to speak.

Jesus always wanted to express the image of God. He did not try to deviate or separate Himself from the

Godhead. And although God the Father, Jesus, and the Holy Spirit are three distinct personalities, each is a component of God. Likewise, my husband and I are two different people, but we're one because of our covenant.

As you represent your husband, you represent your head: "But I would have you know, that the head of every man is Christ; and the head of the woman is the man; and the head of Christ is God" (1 Cor. 11:3). In this context,

> *Established authority is for our benefit.*

head refers to "the person in charge," in other words, the leader, or the one who has authority over the other. This established authority is for our benefit. God has arranged this hierarchy so that we may conduct our lives accordingly.

The Identity Issue

You may be reluctant to submit because you want to establish your own identity. You want to operate independently of your husband. You may think, *Lord, if I submit, who's going to know all the work I put into getting my husband to where he is today? Who's going to give me recognition? Who's going to know that it was really me who helped make it possible for him to succeed?* Honey, it's not about you; it's about the will of the Father.

Jesus did not try to establish His own identity, so why should we? The Word of God says that Jesus "made himself of no reputation, and took upon him the form of a servant" (Phil 2:7). He recognized His purpose on the earth. Let's recognize our purpose as helper by becoming humble and submissive, just as Jesus did. Decide once and for all that you will do whatever it takes to carry out God's plan. God will reward you openly for the things no one else knows about (Matt. 6:4–6).

Our compliance with authority has nothing to do with how we feel. There are times when I don't feel like submitting to Creflo; however, I must follow God's established order, regardless of how I feel. I have come to realize that God has called my husband to lead me, just as Jesus leads the church. The husband-wife relationship is likened to that of Christ and the church. Everything that Jesus instructs us to do is found in the Word, and it demonstrates His love for us. Therefore, marriage should represent the love between Jesus and the church.

The Word of God also instructs us to submit to worldly authority: "Submit yourselves to every ordinance of man for the Lord's sake: whether it be to the king, as supreme; or unto governors" (1 Peter 2:13–14). If we are to submit to worldly authority, how much more should we submit to godly authority?

I thank God that my husband and I are submitted to God's Word and His plan for our lives. If we weren't, we would literally be destroying ourselves. Our lives would be wasted because God's purpose for *us* would not be fulfilled. Sometimes people think that if they neglect to fulfill God's plan for their lives, His plan will stagnate, and the work will never get done. On the contrary, God will find a way to carry out His mission. If I decided to be really foolish and leave World Changers Ministries, the ministry would not collapse. Even if both Creflo and I decided to abandon this vision, it would still go on. God would anoint someone else to carry out His plans. But by not submitting, we would miss out.

We must seek the Lord for His will. Jesus announced, "Ask and keep on asking and it shall be given you; seek and keep on seeking and you shall find; knock and keep on knocking and the door shall be opened to you" (Luke 11:9 AMPLIFIED). Ask the Lord for greater revelation and understanding of how to become the glory of your husband or of Jesus. Seek Him for new ways to represent your man of God. Keep on knocking until you get the answers you seek.

Confession

Make the following confession by choosing one or both of the options within the parentheses.

I thank You, Father, that You have created me for a specific purpose. I thank You that I am the expressed image of (my husband/You), Lord God. I will learn how to be a *good* help to (my husband/You). I will represent (him/You) in an honorable way at all times. When people see me, they will see (my husband/You) because we are one in vision and purpose, and I purpose not to do anything that will jeopardize this covenant. I walk in Your will at all times. I declare this to be so now in Jesus' name. Amen.

Study Questions

1. Do you know God's purpose for your life? If so, how was it revealed to you? If not, what are you doing to find out?

2. Do you hear from God on a daily basis? How do you know it is Him?

3. If you are a married woman, what role do you play in your husband's life? How are you fulfilling your God-appointed role as a help meet (Gen. 2:18)?

4. If you are a single woman, what are the biblical ways in which you can begin to prepare yourself for your future mate, as discussed in this chapter?

5. How well do you represent Jesus? Your spouse?

6. Is the plan you have for your life in agreement with God's plan? In what ways are they in agreement? In what ways do they differ?

7. Why is it important to know God's will for your life?

Challenge

Look at your life, your career, your extracurricular activities, and with God's help determine if you are spending enough time doing the things He has called you to do. Be willing to submit to His direction.

How art thou fallen from heaven, O Lucifer, son of the morning! how art thou cut down to the ground, which didst weaken the nations! For thou hast said in thine heart, I will ascend into heaven, I will exalt my throne above the stars of God: I will sit also upon the mount of the congregation, in the sides of the north: I will ascend above the heights of the clouds; I will be like the most High. Yet thou shalt be brought down to hell, to the sides of the pit.

—Isaiah 14:12–15

7

Living Free from Strife

❧

Do you know how Satan, the once-beautiful cherubim, fell from his wonderful position in heaven? He wanted to be like the most high God. He purposed in his heart to exalt himself and ascend to the throne of God, and yet he was brought down to the pit of hell. Satan desired to be higher than God. In other words, he was operating in strife. In fact, Satan is the father of strife!

Strife is defined as "contention, quarreling, disagreeing, or arguing." In more common terms, it means being just plain hard to get along with. Strife also promotes stress—and who needs that? Another definition for *strife* is "discord or competition, contention for superiority, or selfish ambition." It is the motive behind Satan's entire being. When you begin to exert your thoughts and ways over others', and feel that you are superior to them, you, too, are operating in strife. The same is true when you refuse to settle a disagreement.

Strife begins in a person's heart, but is revealed through words and actions. For this reason, you must guard your heart. How? Be selective in choosing what you see, hear, and say. I am not interested in listening to talk shows every day. Sometimes the discussions on those programs sow seeds of discord in the mind of the viewer. And when the show is over, you're all emotional over something that may not be a reality in your life. You become influenced to the point of believing things contrary to the truth.

> *Be selective in choosing what you see, hear, and say.*

For example, today's show reveals the signs to watch for if you suspect your spouse may be cheating on you. Your own relationship is going just fine, but you remember an argument you had recently or you notice that your husband demonstrated one of the characteristics discussed on the show. When he comes home, all of a sudden you're mad and ready to lash out. And he is asking, "What?"

Strife in the Garden

Satan introduced Adam and Eve to strife in the Garden of Eden. Eve knew perfectly well God's instructions regarding the Tree of Knowledge of Good and Evil. He had already informed her that if she ate of or even touched the tree, she would die. However, Satan sowed a seed of doubt in her mind by challenging God's instructions to her. He said, "Ye shall not surely die: for God doth know that in the day ye eat thereof, then your eyes shall be opened, and ye shall be as gods, knowing good and evil" (Gen. 3:4–5). Satan knew that he would appeal to Eve's desire to know it all—he enticed her to believe that she was wiser than God. He no doubt chose her for that very reason.

As a woman of God, you have to be careful about the reports you see and hear. At times, you just have to shut out some of the information floating around in the world. As a virtuous woman, you must also become more selective about those you converse with. Coworkers, friends, and even family members may not be at your level spiritually. Gossip is all around you, and you must understand that you don't have to know everything about everybody. There are all sorts of lies trying to get you to doubt God's, or even your husband's, words.

In Genesis 3 we discover that Adam and Eve wanted to be on God's level. When the serpent entered the garden and posed the question, "Hath God said?" he got their attention and led them into strife. They began to dispute what God had already told them. They felt that God was keeping valuable information from them. But God really wanted them to pass the test of obedience. They wanted to know what God knew, so the devil tricked them, and their curiosity led them to sin.

Genesis 3:6 adds to the story: "And when the woman saw that the tree was good for food, and that it was pleasant to the eyes, and a tree to be desired to make one wise, she took of the fruit thereof, and did eat, and gave also unto her husband with her; and he did eat." Adam and Eve wanted to be in a place of author-

> *Child of God, the devil is cunning and divisive. He uses the spoken word to lead us into strife.*

ity—a place God had not ordained them to be. Child of God, the devil is cunning and divisive. He uses the spoken word to lead us into strife. On the other hand, God uses the hearing of His Word to lead us into faith. Faith comes by hearing the Word of God (Rom. 10:17).

Strife in Our Time

Now that we know how Satan works, let's consider other ways we allow strife to enter in. Strife originates in your *soul*—"your mind, will, and emotions." It is conceived in your *thoughts* and in your *feelings*—"where you think and feel." However, it is birthed through the words you say.

Here is an example of how strife begins. You've received a bad report from your child's teacher that little Johnny has been disobedient. It has been a long day, and you don't want to hear about his turning over all the chairs in the lunchroom. Initially, you were even offended by the news that your child was disobedient. After all, you teach him well, and you correct him when he is out of line. You think, *Well, if they had more supervision in this school, little Johnny would not have gotten out of hand.* Finally, you feel justified in giving the teacher a piece of your mind. Warning! You've just entered the strife zone. When you act on ungodly thoughts and say things that provoke arguments and disagreement, you operate in strife.

There is a more positive approach to this situation. The Word of God advises us to resist the proud (James 4:6). Instead of operating in pride regarding your child, make it a point to hear the facts first. I didn't say *truth.* The truth about your child is based on the Word of God. However, instead of justifying your child's behavior, respond by saying, "Thank you for sharing that information with me. I will talk with Johnny about his temper to make sure that he doesn't do this again." Even if strife was forming in your heart, your positive approach prevents it from progressing any farther.

Marital and family relationships are two of the devil's prime targets for strife. He uses words and the simple things to get us off track, for example: "I really don't think what you did was right," or "You didn't have to say it like that." Satan often uses these statements to light the fuse that causes strife. Disagreements also present opportunities for strife to begin.

When something is said or done that hurts your feelings, decide right then that you will not allow strife to enter in. Decide that you are going to walk in love and peace, and communicate your feelings to your loved one without holding on to the offense or causing offense.

I guard my heart continuously in my marriage. My husband is very loving and wonderful, but sometimes things happen in our relationship that make my flesh want to rise up against him. That is when submission comes into play, and I must rely on the Word of God. Many times our emotions can become more of a disadvantage than an advantage in relationships and life in general. However, as we practice thinking, saying, and doing what the Word of God commands us to do, we can line up our emotions with the Word of God in every circumstance and avoid a whole lot of strife.

I tend to internalize things. When something happens to me or when something is said to me that I don't necessarily like, I try to figure out why. Sometimes this is not the best thing to do because I may assume the worst. In certain cases, it may be wiser to immediately say what I feel, as long as I use balance, and refuse to say things that I'll later regret.

Oftentimes, I become angry after rehearsing the offenses in my mind. I dwell on what happened, and for the life of me, I can't seem to get past it. This isn't the best idea either. Even after talking to the person I'm angry with or offended by, the best resort may be to agree to disagree, or to disagree agreeably. In other words, although I may not agree with what the other person says, each of us can agree to respect the other's opinion or belief. And that's it! There is no need to revisit that conversation because we'll start arguing again. Think about it: it's ridiculous to become angry with someone because he doesn't see things exactly the way you do.

When you operate in strife, you are vulnerable to operating in all the other works of the flesh:

> Now the works of the flesh are manifest, which are these; adultery, fornication, uncleanness, lasciviousness, idolatry, witchcraft, hatred, variance, emulations, wrath, strife, seditions, heresies, envyings, murders, drunkenness, revellings, and such like: of the which I tell you before, as I have also told you in time past, that they which do such things shall not inherit the kingdom of God. (Gal. 5:19–21)

Strife can become so extreme that it can actually lead a person to murder or suicide. It is not something that can be taken lightly. Think of how many times you've heard news reports of a horrible murder sparked by an argument. There are numerous reports like these, simply because those involved failed to reach an agreement. The spirit of strife can prevent you from entering the kingdom of God (Gal. 5:21), and I certainly don't want an argument or any other form of strife to keep me out of heaven.

The Way to Counteract Strife

As children of God, we must adorn ourselves with the fruit of the Spirit—love, joy, peace, long- suffering, gentleness, goodness, faith, meekness, and temperance (Gal. 5:22). Let's purpose in our hearts to get rid of the strife in our lives and increase our love walk by learning to live and walk in the Spirit. Let's focus more on having an "attitude of gratitude" so that others will see our good works and "glorify [our] Father which is in heaven" (Matt. 5:16).

> *Let's purpose in our hearts to get rid of the strife in our lives and increase our love walk by learning to live and walk in the Spirit.*

Confession

Heavenly Father, I thank You for the understanding that You have given me regarding strife. I will purpose in my heart to avoid strife and every evil work of the flesh. I will reduce the amount of stress in my life, and I will love my family, friends, and all those around me with the love of God. As I think on good things and speak the Word of God only, my life will reflect the fruit of the Spirit—love, joy, peace, patience, gentleness, goodness, faith, meekness, and self-control. I declare this to be so now in Jesus' name. Amen.

Study Questions

1. How easy or difficult is it for you to recognize areas in your life where strife is at work?

2. How do you identify when the devil is deliberately doing things to interrupt your relationships?

3. How frequently do you encounter feelings of stress or anger?

4. Do you spend time trying to discover the root cause of feelings of strife? How much time?

5. How much time do you spend watching soap operas and talk shows?

6. What methods of prevention are you using to strife–proof your home?

7. How often do you and your family pray as a group? Is each member consistent in praying individually and for other members of the family?

Challenge

Be aware of the devil's schemes, and refuse to succumb to his attempts to get you off track. Spend more time in the Word, and allow the love of God to reign supreme in your relationships.

"Strength and dignity are her clothing and her position is strong and secure . . . "

Proverbs 31:25, AMPLIFIED

8

Jezebel and the Power of Influence

~~~~~~~~~

SEVERAL MISCONCEPTIONS EXIST IN THE BODY OF Christ concerning *Jezebel*. Some believe the term refers only to women who wear heavy makeup and excessive jewelry. To others, it immediately brings to mind someone who is considered "loose." My goal is to clarify the origin of this spirit and its methods of operation while exposing the areas where it may be hidden. Perhaps this information will also help you to see the areas in your life where the Jezebel spirit may be at work.

When I began to deal with this subject a few years ago, I realized that some areas in my life had been dominated by the spirit of Jezebel and needed adjusting. Once I exposed them, they had to go. We must reckon with this subject so that we may be covered and kept holy unto God. And we must recognize Satan's agenda and how he operates through the spirit of Jezebel.

Satan dwells in darkness, or sin. Therefore, we must repent daily in order to cleanse areas where the devil might find a foothold. The Bible depicts Satan "as a roaring lion, [that] walketh about, seeking whom he may devour" (1 Peter 5:8). In other words, he searches the earth for someone to use for his purpose and ultimately destroy. Just as the church is the bride of Christ, Jezebel is the bride of Satan. And just as God is no respecter of persons, neither is Satan. He will attach himself to anyone, male or female. However, the Jezebel spirit tends to be more operative in women.

Occasionally, when a sermon is being delivered on a particular subject, our first thought is, *I wish so-and-so were here to hear this*. We fail to realize that God, in His infinite wisdom, orchestrated things so that *we* would be in the service that day because, in most cases, the message is for us. It is intended to give us revelation knowledge or direction on what we must do in certain situations. Likewise, as you read this chapter, judge yourself first, and if you find signs of the Jezebel spirit, don't feel condemned. God is willing and able to deliver you today.

The Jezebel Spirit

The first thing to recognize is that *Jezebel* is not a person, but "a demonic spirit that operates through the power of influence." Although Queen Jezebel is a character mentioned in the Old and New Testaments, most references to Jezebel apply to the character in which one operates. The Jezebel spirit existed long before Queen Jezebel, but because this spirit was extremely evident in her character, the term *Jezebel* was later added to better convey its meaning.

Several characteristics portrayed by the Jezebel spirit can be easily detected. They involve acts that promote self-will, which include manipulation, deception, seduction, rebellion, and craftiness. The ultimate goal of the Jezebel spirit is to destroy the image of God. It usurps authority and works to divide and conquer—particularly in relationships. The Jezebel spirit tries to break agreement. The demonstration of these actions can be either subtle or blatant, and may exist in children as well as in adults.

> *The ultimate goal of the Jezebel spirit is to destroy the image of God.*

Vulnerable Personality Types

Several types of personalities are more vulnerable to this spirit. For example, motivationally gifted individuals are extremely susceptible. They are generally very talented individuals who have a charismatic personality. Often they are Christians who are empowered with the gift of prophetic insight, are knowledgeable in the Word of God, and are filled with the Holy Spirit.

Allow me to elaborate for a moment on prophetic ministry. The spirit of Jezebel is the number one enemy of the prophetic ministry. "Why?" you may ask. The purpose of prophecy is to disclose *revelation knowledge*, which is "knowledge revealed to your born-again spirit by God." Satan doesn't want you to know the truth. He wants you to remain blinded to the reality of God's promises and His perfect will. As long as he is able to keep you from knowing the truth, Satan can continue to distort God's Word and prevent you from fulfilling your purpose in life. The prophet's job is to restore order, or proper respect toward authority. God-man, parent-child, husband-wife, pastor-congregation, and employer-employee relationships fit this category. For this reason, we must be extremely sensitive and refuse to rebel against authority in order to stay in the perfect will of God. Rebellion in any form—thought, deed, or word—will only give place for the devil to operate.

The spirit of Jezebel is aware that it can be recognized easily through the prophetic eye. Nonetheless, it is a seductive and manipulative spirit that thrives on the weaknesses of others. Therefore, those who operate in the gift of prophecy are wise to protect themselves from people and places that promote sexual promiscuity and moral failure. The devil will use anything to distract God's people and destroy His plan.

Another vulnerable personality type is the ruler, or facilitator. This person generally functions in a position of leadership, either in management or in ministry. Those in the body of Christ may serve in the capacity of minister or teacher.

The third personality type vulnerable to the spirit of Jezebel includes those who have been wounded or rejected. Most often these people have been wounded by a person in authority, particularly a parent. One example would be a person who has a difficult time relating to God as her heavenly Father because of the poor example set by her earthly father. In this case, her relationship with God is incomplete, and the success of other relationships is jeopardized.

The Biblical Example

Let's turn to the Bible, which describes a situation that involved the character of Jezebel. Jezebel's husband, Ahab, was interested in purchasing a vineyard in Jezreel, located near his home. He offered to pay the owner, Naboth, for it or give him a better vineyard. However, Naboth was not interested in selling the property because he had inherited the land. During that time, it was disrespectful to sell anything your father gave you as a gift or an inheritance. Ahab went home depressed about the whole thing and refused to eat.

When Jezebel asked what was wrong, he told her. He began to pout and act like a spoiled child because he didn't get what he wanted. However, Jezebel settled in her mind that *she* would get the land for her husband: "Dost thou now govern the kingdom of Israel? arise, and eat bread, and let thine heart be merry: I will give thee the vineyard of Naboth" (1 Kings 21:7). In essence, she said, "I'll take care of it. Don't worry about it. After all, you are the king of Samaria."

Jezebel proceeded with her plot to take the land from Naboth. She manipulated the elders and nobles of the city by writing them a letter sealed with the king's seal and signed with his name. I believe that's called forgery, right? Anyway, Jezebel arranged for two men to lie about Naboth by saying they heard him blaspheme God and the king. She then commanded the men to stone him to death. Here's what happened next:

And it came to pass, when Jezebel heard that Naboth was stoned, and was dead, that Jezebel said to Ahab, Arise, take possession of the vineyard of Naboth the Jezreelite, which he refused to give thee for money: for

Naboth is not alive, but dead. And it came to pass, when Ahab heard that Naboth was dead, that Ahab rose up to go down to the vineyard of Naboth the Jezreelite, to take possession of it. (1 Kings 21:15–16)

After that incident, the Lord sent Elijah to Ahab to reprimand him for selling out to the devil and for allowing his wife to stir up such evil. The Lord also revealed more to Elijah concerning Ahab and Jezebel: "In the place where dogs licked the blood of Naboth shall dogs lick thy blood . . . And of Jezebel also spake the LORD, saying, The dogs shall eat Jezebel by the wall of Jezreel" (1 Kings 21:19, 23).

Now I ask you, did it take all that? Was having the land worth taking Naboth's life? Certainly not! However, this story gives you some idea of Jezebel's influence. She used her position as queen to manipulate those men to lie about Naboth. She demonstrated how deceptive and crafty she was when she wrote the letter to the elders and forged her husband's signature. Even worse, Jezebel believed her actions were justified.

The Ahab Spirit

For many years, women have taken on the leadership role in the home. And while we have the ability to lead, it is not our role to be the head of the household. God has given the position of headship to men and the job of help to women. Unfortunately when men fail to lead, or there is no man to lead, we are sometimes forced to do the job. Such was the position of Ahab and Jezebel. Rather than handle the matter himself, he allowed his wife to resolve the issue. However, God held Ahab accountable for his wife's actions.

It is extremely important that we stay in the right position. Had this couple been in their God-given positions, things would have turned out differently. Jezebel orchestrated the entire event. She was totally out of order. She didn't help Ahab with *his* plan; instead, Jezebel created one of her own.

The only way for a Jezebel spirit to reach the maximum level of maturity in marriage is for the Ahab spirit to exist. Ahab demonstrated a spirit of irresponsibility. He surrendered his authority to his wife. Men who lack the courage and diligence to see matters through to the end generally dump their responsibility on someone else. In essence, they say, "You handle it." Ahab should have told Jezebel, "I'll handle it."

> *While the Ahab spirit rejects its place of authority, the Jezebel spirit usurps authority.*

While the Ahab spirit rejects its place of authority, the Jezebel spirit usurps authority. When these spirits operate together, they bring doom and the judgment of God. They defy His order.

If the Jezebel spirit is operating in your marriage, or if you notice that many of your family members operate in the spirit of Jezebel, somewhere along the way someone failed to take on the proper role of responsibility. You may remember your dad, your uncle, or even your grandfather having a lackadaisical attitude. Perhaps he lacked the courage to make decisions and passed the responsibility to the woman of the house. Maybe he refused to work, handle the bills, discipline the children, or set the example as the prayer warrior in the home. Whatever the reason, it doesn't matter. A man's job is to cover his family—it is not his wife's responsibility!

One of the things that attracted me to Creflo when we were dating was his leadership ability. I consider myself pretty independent, but I wanted someone who could lead me. Since I've known him, Creflo has never been afraid to stand up for what he believes. We met in college in the early eighties. Many of the people I knew were partying, smoking, and getting drunk. I was eager to know more about God, and I heard about the Bible study that Creflo was teaching on campus. He really stood out as a bright light for Christ. The fact that he chose to stand up for Christ when so many others were following the crowd really attracted me. He had a great impact on my life and on the lives of many others.

Even the Strong May Fall

The spirit of influence also operated in the lives of Samson and Delilah. Samson is known as the strongest man to ever live; however, his greatest weakness was his desire for beautiful women. At the beginning of Judges 16, Samson went to the city of Gaza where he met, and had intercourse with, a prostitute. Expecting that he would stay until morning, the Gazites planned to capture and kill him the next day. Samson learned of their plot and slipped out around midnight.

Shortly thereafter, Samson met a Philistine woman named Delilah, and the Word of God says he loved her. The lords of the Philistines wanted to know the source of Samson's strength, so they asked Delilah to entice him. They agreed to pay her several pieces of silver (now valued at more than $140,000). She accepted the offer, and the manipulation process began: "And Delilah said to Samson, Tell me, I pray thee, wherein thy great strength lieth, and wherewith thou mightest be bound to afflict thee" (Judg. 16:6). In other words, "What makes you so strong, and what does it take to subdue you?"

Samson teased her several times by giving answers that he knew would never work. She became impatient, but she refused to let up. After all, $140,000 is nothing to sneeze at. Delilah continued to nag him every day until he finally became so weary and annoyed that he told her the truth.

And when Delilah saw that he had told her all his heart, she sent and called for the lords of the Philistines, saying, Come up this once, for he hath shewed me all his heart. Then the lords of the Philistines came up unto her, and brought money in their hand. And she made him sleep upon her knees; and she called for a man, and she caused him to shave off the seven locks of his head; and she began to afflict him, and his strength went from him. (Judg. 16:18–19)

Continue reading this chapter, and you will find that was the beginning of the end for Samson. The Philistines took him prisoner and blinded him as punishment. However, God allowed him to avenge himself on his enemies. When the Philistine lords gathered to offer a sacrifice to their god, Samson leaned on the supporting pillars of the temple and the structure collapsed, killing everyone inside, including himself (Judg. 16:21–30).

Proverbs 7 issues a warning for men who get involved with loose women. The end result is always death, either spiritual or physical. Delilah's greed and Samson's failure to operate in wisdom cost him his life. Many women are like Delilah: they play the game until they get what they want. But women should never act out of selfish motives. The influence demonstrated by women who operate under the spirit of Jezebel is often used as a tool for control and selfish ambition.

God-Directed Influence

As a virtuous woman of God, you cannot afford to operate under this selfish spirit, of influence. Your influence should be God-directed. The love of God in you and the godly character you portray should be your only sources of influence. Your very existence should motivate others to become more like Christ. Your impact on others should be so great that they are better for having known you.

> *Your impact on others should be so great that they are better for having known you.*

You have the ability to be either a positive or a negative influence in your relationships. In other words, you have the power to be either a benefit or a detriment. Whether it is a relationship with your child, spouse, parents, family, or friends, God has positioned you where you are with a major purpose in mind. That purpose is to somehow use you to build and establish His kingdom.

When you make a decision to live according to the Word of God, your relationships become more of what God intended. The Bible tells us that whatever we sow, we will also reap (Gal. 6:7). Likewise, the influence you sow will produce the influence you gain. Make sure you give what you expect to receive. And in everything, live to please God.

Confession

Lord God, thank You for helping me to better understand the spirit of Jezebel. If there are areas in my life where the spirit of Jezebel is at work, reveal them to me so that I may quickly make the necessary adjustments. I purpose to use my influence in a positive manner by allowing Your light to shine through me in all that I do. I declare this to be so now in Jesus' name. Amen.

Study Questions

1. Do you think the spirit of Ahab or Jezebel is at work in your life? What characteristics of this spirit do you display?

2. How often do you capitalize on the weaknesses of others?

3. Are you controlling, manipulative, or overly aggressive?

4. Which of the personality types described as susceptible to the Jezebel spirit (motivationally gifted, leader/facilitator, or wounded/rejected) do you possess, if any?

5. If you are married, are you and your husband operating effectively in your God-appointed positions or are you misplaced? What evidence do you have to prove this?

6. Do others consider you more of a positive or a negative influence in their lives?

7. How often are you motivated by personal gain?

Challenge

Make a decision to become a godly influence to everyone! If you have a domineering spirit, seek God for direction on how to change. Spend more time with Him, and remember to listen more and talk less in your prayers.

"Again I say unto you, That if two of you shall agree on earth as touching any thing that they shall ask, it shall be done for them of my Father which is in heaven"

Matthew 18:19

9

The Power of Agreement

⤙~⤚

IT IS IMPORTANT THAT WE AS BELIEVERS UNDERSTAND the power made available to us through agreement. Prayer is one of the most important areas in the life of a Christian. It is our lifeline, our method of daily communication with the Father. Through prayer, God reveals things to the spirit man. Jesus spoke of this power:

Verily I say unto you, Whatsoever ye shall bind on earth shall be bound in heaven: and whatsoever ye shall loose on earth shall be loosed in heaven. Again I say unto you, That if two of you shall agree on earth as touching any thing that they shall ask, it shall be done for them of my Father which is in heaven. For where two or three are gathered together in my name, there am I in the midst of them. (Matt. 18:18–20)

This passage begins with Jesus telling His disciples that whatever is *bound,* or "tied up," on earth is also bound in heaven. This principle also applies to *loosing,* or "releasing," things on earth—the same is done in heaven. Now don't get too spiritual with this. You can't go around binding things that are not in agreement with the Word of God. I've heard people trying to bind things like pollen, and you just can't do that. The only thing you can do is bind the effects of pollen on your body. Not everything has a demon or demonic spirit behind it. Amen? Amen! Notice the language of The Amplified Bible: "whatever you forbid and declare to be improper and unlawful on earth must be what is already forbidden in heaven, and whatever you permit and declare proper and lawful on earth must be what is already permitted in heaven" (v. 18).

In verse 19 of the same passage in the King James Version, Jesus continued to speak about the mechanics of agreement: "That if two of you shall agree on earth as touching any thing that they shall ask, it shall be done for them of my Father." I've watched some people jump off the deep end with this one. They'll grab someone's hand and say, "Let's touch and agree." The next thing you know, you've got a bunch of people concentrating more on touching than on agreement. That is not the correct interpretation of this Scripture. Agreement involves more than just holding someone's hand.

The word *agreement* means "to be in harmony or to symphonize in spirit, soul, and body." In other words, it means being one with another person in whatever is being lifted up in prayer or believing God for the same result as the other person believes. I like the way that The Amplified Bible explains it: "If two of you on earth agree (harmonize together, make a symphony together) about whatever [anything and everything] they may ask, it will come to pass and be done for them by My Father in heaven." Agreement brings God into the picture. Jesus promised that He will dwell in the midst of those who are in agreement (v. 20). His job is to carry out whatever is being agreed upon.

> *Jesus promised that He will dwell in the midst of those who are in agreement.*

I encourage you to write on paper your prayers of agreement and sign them along with your prayer partner. (A prayer partner is someone with whom you pray frequently, someone who adds her agreement to yours in prayer.) Many times we tell someone that we will agree with him or her in prayer and then forget what we have just committed ourselves to. Think about it: you promise to agree with someone, but before long, it slips your mind.

There is only so much that the human mind can retain. However, when you write your prayers of agreement, you'll forget less and remember more. Writing them anchors your mind to the truth of God's Word and increases your faith.

Here is an example of a written prayer of agreement:

Father, we ask in the name of Jesus [state your petition]. Satan, we notify you in this agreement that you are hereby bound, and you will not function, operate, harass, embarrass, or intimidate us because this agreement lines up with the Word of God according to [insert a Scripture reference]. Satan, we render you helpless in this matter. We believe it is done now, in Jesus' name. Amen.

Keep the paper in a place where you can see it so that you and your partner will be reminded daily of your agreement.

Agreement with Your Spouse

If there are two people on earth who should always agree in prayer, it is a wife and her husband. You and your spouse should agree on the things you are believing God for, whether it is a new job or promotion, a new house or car, children, or debt cancellation. As long as your prayers line up with the Word of God, your agreement immediately unleashes the miracle-working power of God. We learn from Deuteronomy 32:30 that "one [can] chase a thousand, and two put ten thousand to flight." One righteous person can do a lot of damage to Satan's kingdom, but two righteous people in agreement with God can destroy it!

But if your house is filled with animosity, strife, and resentment, the power of agreement becomes ineffective and is unable to bring about your manifestation. According to 1 Peter 3:7 (AMPLIFIED), husbands are commanded to live in peace with their wives, so their prayers will not be hindered:

> In the same way you married men should live considerately with [your wives], with an intelligent recognition [of the marriage relation], honoring the woman as [physically] the weaker, but [realizing that you] are joint heirs of the grace (God's unmerited favor) of life, in order that your prayers may not be hindered and cut off. [Otherwise you cannot pray effectively.]

In this verse, Paul stressed the importance of harmony between husband and wife. The wife should submit to her husband as she would submit to Christ. Do not disrespect or dishonor your husband by nagging and criticizing him all the time. Instead, allow him to be the head so that your prayers will not be hindered. As he strives to follow God, agree with him in prayer.

"But, Sister Taffi," you may say, "I'm not married. What does all this have to do with me?" Everything! The same principle applies to your life. In 1 Corinthians 7:32–35, Paul instructed single men and women to submit themselves to God for their own benefit, so that they might concentrate on serving Him, and allow Christ to be the head of their lives. Married or single, we must walk in love so that God can mold us into vessels fit for His use.

> *Married or single, we must walk in love so that God can mold us into vessels fit for His use.*

Powerful Weapons of the Enemy

It is a shame that more of us do not tap into the power of agreement. We choose instead to entertain strife, envy, and unforgiveness without realizing the damage these sins can cause in our lives and the lives of others. And unless we examine our hearts carefully for sin—especially in the areas of strife, envy, and unforgiveness—we shouldn't expect to receive anything from God. Why? These attitudes can hinder and block our prayers altogether.

Too many times we try to bury these ungodly attitudes inside ourselves, thinking that we are hiding them from God. The reality is that we are fooling ourselves. Honey, you can never fool God. He sees everything! Our actions

> *It is up to you, Child of God, to work with the Holy Spirit.*

always give us away. Jesus said that Christians are recognized by the fruit we bear (Matt. 7:16). Fruit, in this context, refers to the fruit of the Spirit described in Galatians 5. We should rid ourselves of anything that would hinder us from hearing and receiving from God.

Strife, envy, and unforgiveness are three of the most powerful weapons of the enemy. Unchecked, they have the power to build strongholds in your life and cancel out your prayers. It is up to you, Child of God, to work with the Holy Spirit and allow Him to point out the areas in your life where these attitudes have become entrenched. His job is to lead you into all truth by pointing out the very things that hinder your fellowship with God. Your mind and spirit must be cleansed daily; otherwise, the devil will have an opportunity to get a foothold.

Unforgiveness

The word *unforgiveness* means "to refuse to overlook a transgression or release a person from debt." "Release from debt? Sister Taffi, he didn't owe me any money. What are you talking about?" Child of God, debt is not limited to finances. If someone hurts your feelings, don't you feel that he *owes* you an apology? Anytime something is taken away from you, it is owed to you; therefore, it becomes a debt that another has to pay. Before Jesus died, mankind owed a debt of atonement to God. In Old Testament times, people were commanded to burn sacrifices for the atonement, or forgiveness, of sin. That is why we say, "Jesus paid our debts in full." He was the perfect sacrifice. In the same way, when someone comes to you and asks for forgiveness, you are obligated to forgive him.

> For if you forgive people their trespasses [their reckless and willful sins, leaving them, letting them go, and giving up resentment], your heavenly Father will also forgive you. But if you do not forgive others their trespasses [their reckless and willful sins, leaving them, letting them go, and giving up resentment], neither will your Father forgive you your trespasses. (Matt. 6:14–15 AMPLIFIED)

The problem occurs when you say, "I'll forgive you, but I won't forget what you did!" That is the kind of prayer-hindering attitude I'm talking about. True forgiveness means complete debt cancellation, no strings attached. I realize that forgiving someone can be difficult. However, it is the requirement we must satisfy to be forgiven by God.

Not forgiving someone can be detrimental. "But you don't know what he did to me!" Child of God, it doesn't matter what the offense was. The important thing is that you forgive the offender, even if he hasn't asked for forgiveness: "And whenever you stand praying, if you have anything against anyone, forgive him and let it drop (leave it, let it go), in order that your Father Who is in heaven may also forgive you your [own] failings and shortcomings and let them drop" (Mark 11:25 AMPLIFIED).

How important is God's forgiveness to you? I take His forgiveness very seriously. I want to be sure that when I make a mistake, God will forgive me immediately and not hold anything against me. That's what walking in love is all about. It's forgiving others even when they haven't asked you to and when you don't feel like it.

Envy

Envy is another problem area. To *envy* means to "have ill will" toward someone. In other words, you get upset when someone other than yourself receives favor, promotion, or blessings from God. James indicated that "wherever there is jealousy (envy) and contention (rivalry and selfish ambition), there will also be confusion (unrest, disharmony, rebellion) and all sorts of evil and vile practices" (James 3:16 AMPLIFIED). You can have breakfast with the angels every morning, yet your prayers of agreement may be hindered because of envy.

God desires to pour blessings upon all of His children. He is not a respecter of persons, but of faith. You don't know how long or how hard that a person has been praying to receive from God. You certainly don't know everything he has been through. My husband and I say it this way: "Never judge a person's harvest unless you know the kind of seed he has

If someone is blessed, rejoice with him!

sown." The Bible commands us in Romans 12:15 to "rejoice with them that do rejoice." In other words, if someone is blessed, rejoice with him! Share in the happiness! That simple act of obedience could be the key to *your* breakthrough. When you rejoice with others, you are one step closer to receiving the blessings you are believing God for.

Strife

An attitude of envy will always lead to strife. The Bible tells us that strife comes as a result of not getting our own way:

What leads to strife (discord and feuds) and how do conflicts (quarrels and fightings) originate among you? Do they not arise from your sensual desires that are ever warring in your bodily members? You are jealous and covet [what others have] and your desires go unfulfilled; [so] you become murderers. [To hate is to murder as far as your hearts are concerned.] You burn with envy and anger and are not able to obtain [the gratification, the contentment, and the happiness that you seek], so you fight and war. You do not have, because you do not ask. (James 4:1–2 AMPLIFIED)

Envy ushers in the spirit of strife. They work on a tag-team system. You become jealous of someone else's blessing, then you begin to treat the person differently. Before you realize what's happening, strife has entered in and caused division between the two of you. This happens many times in marriage. For example, one spouse may get a promotion and make more money than the other. The other spouse gets jealous and feels threatened. When all is said and done, you have dissension between two people who are supposed to be joined together to defeat the devil rather than allow him to steal their peace. And it's not limited to marital relationships. Strife can enter into any relationship and cause just as much damage. It is a very subtle enemy, which is why it is important to uncover how this spirit works.

At times you may become so irritable and upset that you don't want to have anything to do with God. You find it hard to pray and virtually impossible to enter into God's presence when strife is in your heart. Praying in agreement may be the last thing you want to do when you're angry with someone. But you can't be in strife and expect the power of agreement to work on your behalf. Strife will cancel out your prayers—just like that!

When I began to understand the power of agreement, I noticed that strife was trying to get a foothold in my life. It seemed as if the least little things would upset me and cause me to get spiritually off track. I now realize that Satan tries to use strife to hinder my prayers of agreement with Creflo. I know that it is just a matter of time before those things we're believing God for manifest. Therefore, I deliberately try to avoid anything that would prevent that from happening.

Make a decision not to allow the spirit of strife to enter into your relationships. Understand, however, that it's not going to be easy to follow through on your decision because certain people know how to push your buttons. Instead of dwelling on the problem, settle the fact in your heart and mind, and refuse to get into strife, regardless of the situation. If you have to keep your mouth shut and leave the room, do it. Just don't give the devil a foothold.

Look to Jesus

Unforgiveness, envy, and strife are not luxuries you and I can afford to walk in. We all have things that we are believing God for. But they will never come to pass unless we do as Paul commanded in the twelfth chapter of Hebrews:

Therefore we also, since we are surrounded by so great a cloud of witnesses, let us lay aside every weight, and

the sin which so easily ensnares us, and let us run with
endurance the race that is set before us, looking unto
Jesus, the author and finisher of our faith, who for the
joy that was set before Him endured the cross, despis-
ing the shame, and has sat down at the right hand of
the throne of God. (vv. 1–2 NKJV)

The Christian faith requires discipline. Paul said that
we have to let go of the unnecessary weight of envy, strife,
and unforgiveness if we are ever going to reach the finish
line in heaven. Discipline is hard work, but the rewards
are endless. So I encour-
age you to search your
heart and judge yourself.
If you don't have a
prayer partner—some-
one to agree with you in

> *I will continue to
> wait in faith for the
> manifestation of
> my prayers.*

prayer—ask God to send someone your way who lives
according to His Word.

Whatever you do, don't pray in agreement and then
speak against your prayer. Place a guard over your mouth,
and wait patiently for the manifestation. The Bible promises us that as we are transformed by the renewing of our
minds, we will be able to "prove . . . what is the good and
acceptable and perfect will of God, even the thing which
is good and acceptable and perfect [in His sight for you]"
(Rom. 12:2 AMPLIFIED).

Confession

Father, in the name of Jesus, I thank You that I have what I say when I pray in agreement with Your Word. I thank You for the power that comes from praying in agreement, and I deliberately place a guard over my heart and mouth right now, to avoid saying things that would cancel out my prayers. Instead, I will continue to wait in faith for the manifestation of my prayers. I thank You for the ability to live in peace with those around me, and I renounce any strife, unforgiveness, or envy I may be harboring toward anyone. I repent right now, and I receive Your forgiveness. I declare this to be so now in Jesus' name. Amen.

Study Questions

1. Is there something missing, broken, or lacking in your life? How much peace do you really have?

2. Do you have a prayer partner? If so, is he or she committed to fulfilling God's will? If not, what character traits will you look for in a potential partner?

3. Do you rejoice when others prosper, or do you struggle with an "it's not fair" attitude?

4. Are you aware of issues concerning unforgiveness, envy, strife, and bitterness in your life that needs to be addressed and repaired? In what areas? How do you intend to resolve these feelings?

5. Do you try more to make your point or to reach agreement in the middle of an argument?

6. Do you forgive others as freely as God forgives you? Why or why not?

7. How can you do a better job of guarding your heart and mouth?

Challenge

Look for opportunities to agree continuously. It will reduce the number of arguments and add more beauty to your life.

"Wherefore be ye not unwise, but understanding what the will of the Lord is."

Ephesians 5:17

10

Walking in the Will of God

~

EVERY CHRISTIAN SHOULD STRIVE TO KNOW HOW TO walk in the will of God. It should not be a secret or a mystery to us. God wants us to be able to recognize and operate in His will every day of our lives. The Bible tells us, "See then that ye walk circumspectly, not as fools, but as wise, redeeming the time, because the days are evil. Wherefore be ye not unwise, but understanding what the will of the Lord is" (Eph. 5:15–17). Why? So that we can enjoy the blessings of God—the abundant life Jesus spoke of in John 10:10—and avoid the pitfalls that come from disobedience.

Walk Circumspectly

Too many Christians today presume to know the will of God for their lives. Instead of praying and seeking God for direction, they assume roles for themselves. I've heard people say, "I'm called to the ministry," and then struggle with finances, marriage, and the people they serve until they become discouraged and weary in well-doing. According to the Word of God, we are to walk *circumspectly*, or "cautiously, carefully, and prudently." We should be cautious of the things we do and the choices we make, always considering the possible consequences.

To *understand* means "to piece together as with the pieces of a jigsaw puzzle; to comprehend, grasp, or be familiar with." To understand the Lord's will is to piece it together or to make sense of it. It is something that has to be discerned. The only way to do that is to develop a relationship with the Father by listening to Him, talking to Him, and obeying Him.

Contrary to what you may think, the will of God is not something that you can learn all at once, from A to Z. It is actually a steady unfolding of revelation—like Christmas presents that are unwrapped one at a time. The key to receiving this revelation is found in simple acts of

> *The will of God is actually a steady unfolding of revelation.*

obedience. It's like a jigsaw puzzle; once it is completed, the pieces create an entire picture that could not be discerned when the pieces were separated. As we operate in obedience, we will begin to see clearly what God has called us to do.

I remember when the Lord began to deal with me about this subject. I was afraid to yield myself to God because I wasn't sure where He would lead me. I told Him, "Lord, if I yield myself to You, I don't know what might happen!" But as I renewed my mind, the Lord showed me that it was important for me to trust Him and that He had my best interests in mind.

You need to get rid of any fear or pride that may be in your heart. Your attitude and mind-set can hinder you in recognizing God's will. Fear is a spirit that will keep you from progressing in God. It will immobilize you and cause you to doubt. Pride will also keep you from progressing in your Christian walk. It will cause you to rebel and go your own way rather than submit to God.

God's Perfect Will

Elevating your *self-will* above God's *will* leads to God's *permissive will*. In God's permissive will, we make all the choices and often end up making mistakes and hurting ourselves. However, it's never too late to change. If you repent and yield yourself to God's will, He will forgive you and lead you back to the place where He wants you to be—in His perfect will.

Permissive will is when God allows you to carry out your plans. You see, God will never force you to do anything. If He did, the entire world would be saved, and Jesus would have returned by now. Although it is God's will for everyone to be saved (1 Tim. 2:4), He will not force anyone to accept salvation. It is a free gift. Either you choose to receive the gift, or you don't. The same is true of the will of God. He will reveal it to you if you're willing to listen. And His will for your life will come to pass only if you're willing to obey Him.

> *His will for your life will come to pass only if you're willing to obey Him.*

I experienced this very thing while I was in college. I took a job that required me to work at night. My goal was to earn money to pay for school and to buy the things I needed. However, my plan failed because it was not the job that God wanted me to have. Since I worked at night, I was always tired, and I could barely accomplish anything. I finally realized that I was not living in God's perfect will for my life. I was in His permissive will, and I had to repent.

When you are out of the perfect will of God, things just aren't right. If you are always struggling to make ends meet, or if you are without peace, there is a good chance that you are doing things that are out of God's perfect will. Just when it seems you're getting ahead, you go into reverse again. Many times you really aren't happy. You may look happy and sometimes fool yourself. But the truth is, you'd rather be doing something else.

Now don't get me wrong. Just because that job in college wasn't God's will for me doesn't mean that it wasn't God's will for someone else. His plan for me is not His plan for you. Not everyone can be a lawyer, a teacher, or an accountant. It requires a lot of energy to fake your way. You have to "perpetrate" and try to force things to happen. If it doesn't come naturally, you may need to check yourself. "Well, I'm anointed to do all things," you may say. Honey, you may be anointed, but the Word says you have to be willing and *able*. You can be willing to sing in the choir, but are you *able* to sing? Can you even carry a tune? If I tried to be a surgeon, I'd do more harm than good because God didn't call me to be a surgeon.

God has a plan and a purpose for everyone. But we must be careful not to get weighed down by selfish desires. It's not about what we want; it's about what God wants. We read in Proverbs 3:5–6, "Trust in the LORD with all thine heart; and lean not unto thine own understanding. In all thy ways acknowledge him, and he shall direct thy paths." And the next verse adds, "Be not wise in thine own eyes" (v. 7). God has created each person to do a specific task. Trust Him because He sees the big picture.

You must understand and accept the perfect will of God for your life. When you are carrying out God's assignment, you are under His protection. So if anything goes wrong or you run out of resources, God's got your back. In other words, God is ready to support and defend you. My husband says, "Your provision is on the other side of your obedience." If God tells you to do something, and you commit yourself to do it, He will provide whatever you need to get the job done. Healing, debt cancellation, deliverance, wisdom, and anything else you need are made available to you when you walk in God's will.

The Importance of Spiritual Perception

Problems come when we allow self-will to dictate a course of action. However, when we yield to the Spirit of God, we see things as God does. This is known as perception. When God reveals something through your spirit, and you act on it, that's perception. Your mind may not comprehend why you're doing it, but in your heart you know it's the right thing to do. Perception is an important aspect of understanding the will of God. It is also an important aspect of operating in the gift of discernment. Oftentimes certain situations and circumstances require you to see with spiritual eyes rather than natural eyes.

The Shunammite woman in 2 Kings understood that Elisha was a prophet of God. She didn't regard him as a "fat cat" breezing through town; instead she allowed God to show her that he was an anointed man of God. She had never seen the man before, and she knew nothing of him. Yet she said unto her husband, "Behold now, I perceive that this is an holy man of God, which passeth by us continually. Let us make a little chamber, I pray thee, on the wall . . . and it shall be, when he cometh to

> *As children of God, we should make decisions based on spiritual perception rather than natural observance.*

us, that he shall turn in thither" (2 Kings 4:9–10). The woman saw Elisha as a prophet of God, and she made room for him in her house. Her perception later paid off when her son died suddenly and Elisha revived him. Because the Shunammite woman was obedient to the prompting of God, she received His provision for her son.

This same principle can be applied to us today. As children of God, we should make decisions based on spiritual perception rather than natural observance. For example, suppose you have a high-paying job, a beautiful three-story home, cars, and all the material possessions you desire. If God asked you to move to Kansas to get involved in a ministry there, what would you do? "Well, Sister Taffi, I don't know about that. I'd have to be sure it was God." You are absolutely right. But what if it was God? Would you be prepared to leave your comfort zone in order to line up with God's will for your life? Or would you take the chance of missing the will of God and suffer the consequences?

Your Covenant Agreement with God

When you walk in the will of God, your will agrees with His will. And to know His will, you must read the written Word of God and consistently spend time in His presence. God has a way of revealing things to you through your spirit. You can get the ball rolling by demonstrating your willingness to fulfill His plan for your life. He promises that if you will hear Him and obey His commandments, His blessings will overtake you (Deut. 28:2). This is your covenant agreement with God.

Ask yourself, Am I in God's will right now? Am I following the lead of my self-will or God's will? You see, God has a plan for you; however, if you make excuses and neglect to do your part, you will miss out on the blessings He longs to give you.

Once you begin to walk in the will of God, don't think that life will become a bed of roses. There will be a few thorns here and there. You may think, *Will this really work?* or, *Things were easier before.* That may be true. But the benefits of walking in the perfect will of God far outweigh any rewards you've ever received by doing things your way. Satan will even use people to distract you.

> *The best way to renew your mind is to increase your personal time with God by studying the Word.*

Don't give in. You may receive criticism from family members or coworkers who don't understand. Just stay focused.

To continue walking in His perfect will, you must renew your mind. Of course, relaxing and taking time away from your daily routine is one way. However, the best way to renew your mind is to increase your personal time with God by studying the Word. Paul urged us, "Do not be conformed to this world, but be transformed by the renewing of your mind, that you may prove what is that good and acceptable and perfect will of God" (Rom. 12:2 NKJV). The more time you spend in God's presence, the more He will reveal to you, and the better you will recognize His voice.

Remember to use God's Word in your prayers, and expect Him to respond. John presented this truth: "And this is the confidence that we have in him, that, if we ask any thing according to his will, he heareth us: and if we know that he hear us, whatsoever we ask, we know that we have the petitions that we desired of him" (1 John 5:14–15). God hears and He will answer. Prayer is having a conversation with God. He talks and you listen. You talk and He listens.

In your prayer time, I encourage you to begin to listen more. Often, God is ready to reveal the answer to you right away. But as soon as you finish talking, you whisk off to the next thing. Off to work, off to church, off to carry out your plans. Then you wonder, *Is He really listening?* The better question would be, "Are you?"

Write the Vision

When God reveals His plan to you—and He will—write it down. Consider the experience of Habakkuk: "The LORD answered me, and said, Write the vision, and make it plain upon tables, that he may run that readeth it" (Hab. 2:2). Writing the vision down assures you that there is a plan for your

> *Whatever your assignment, God's plan is to use it for the building of His kingdom.*

life. Keeping it before your eyes serves as a constant reminder that you should be doing something daily toward accomplishing the task. Therefore, post it on things you use frequently—your refrigerator, mirror, car, doorway, light switch, and computer. It may also be a good idea to frame it and place it on your desk. Not only does it keep you mindful of the vision; it also gives understanding to those who support you. Write the vision clearly. God will send laborers to help accomplish the goal, and they must have a clear understanding of how they may assist you in getting the job done.

It is vitally important that you realize that the vision is not for you. The vision is primarily to benefit others. Whatever your assignment, God's plan is to use it for the building of His kingdom. He wants souls saved and prosperity to abound for each of His children. This is no place for selfish motives. God wants to use you to edify others until all come together in the body of Christ (Eph. 4:11–13).

My husband and I didn't begin World Changers Ministries for our benefit. We certainly didn't decide to go into the ministry to pay off our bills or to become rich. Those were the benefits of being in God's will. God gave my husband the vision to spread the gospel, save souls, change lives, and leave a mark that cannot be erased. Here is the complete vision:

As we proclaim Jesus, the Christ, as Head of the church
and the manifested Word of God, our goal is to teach

the Word of God with simplicity and understanding, so that it may be applied to our everyday lives in a practical and effective manner, thereby being transformed into "World Changers," changing our immediate world and all those with whom we come in contact, ultimately making a mark that cannot be erased.

If you already know God's will for your life and you are walking in it, praise God! If you know His will and you're not actively working toward fulfilling your calling, I encourage you to begin. On the other hand, if you don't know God's will for your life, ask, and you shall receive, so that your joy may be full (John 16:24).

Confession

Heavenly Father, I give my life to You completely to fulfill Your perfect plan. I repent for allowing fear and pride into my life, and for allowing my will to usurp Yours. You know what's best for me, and I trust You. I make a decision to align my will with Yours. I commit to spend more time with You, and I will be more conscious of Your desire to talk to me when I pray. I declare this to be so now in Jesus' name. Amen.

Study Questions

1. Do you base your decisions on past experiences, the experiences and opinions of others, or on God's Word?

2. In what ways does doubt prevent you from going all out for Jesus?

3. Are you quick to obey God, or do you often delay?

4. How frequently do you judge others? Do you judge yourself as frequently or as harshly?

5. Are you living in God's perfect will or His permissive will? How can you tell?

6. How does God alert your spirit?

7. Do you know how to operate in the spirit of perception?

8. Do you operate in the spirit of perception frequently, sometimes, or infrequently? List three instances in which you operated in the spirit of perception.

Challenge

Begin now to consult God first before making any decisions in your life. He promises to direct you in the path that you should go when you acknowledge Him first.

"As for God, his way is perfect: the word of the Lord is tried . . . "

Psalm 18:30

11

The Final Authority

THE WORD OF GOD TELLS US THAT THERE ARE MANY different levels of authority. The Bible is full of stories concerning angels, demons, and earthly rulers. The Amplified Bible informs us that "we are not wrestling with flesh and blood [contending only with physical opponents], but against the despotisms, against the powers, against [the master spirits who are] the world rulers of this present darkness, against the spirit forces of wickedness in the heavenly (supernatural) sphere" (Eph. 6:12).

These principalities operate on a certain level of power; however, 1 Peter 3:22 (AMPLIFIED) states that they are subject to Jesus: "[And He] has now entered into heaven and is at the right hand of God, with [all] angels and authorities and powers made subservient to Him."

The Word of God

Jesus is the Word of God made flesh. The first chapter of John's gospel makes that very clear. We also know that He has been given "all power . . . in heaven and in earth" (Matt. 28:18). The Amplified Bible says all authority has been given to Him. The first definition of the word *authority* is "the power of one whose will and commands must be obeyed by others." That is, someone with authority has the power to cause things to happen. If we know that Jesus is the Word of God, and that He has been given all authority in heaven and earth, then it makes sense to say that the written Word of God has the same authority as Jesus. The Word of God can heal, deliver, promote, make wealthy, and give peace. It has the power to change situations and circumstances.

> *Your choices and decisions should always be subject to the Word of God.*

For this reason, the Bible should be the final authority in our lives. God has provided the answer to every problem and situation in His Word. Our job is to study it and apply the Word to our specific needs through prayer and confession.

The second definition of *authority* is "a ruling or decision." Your choices and decisions should always be subject to the Word of God. The Bible should have authority in every area of your life, from finances to child rearing. It doesn't matter if you wake up singing with the angels every morning; if the decisions you make and the advice you receive do not line up with the Word of God, they are wrong. Too many times we allow our past experiences to dictate to us how we should live rather than choose to trust and live by the Word of God: "As for God, his way is perfect: the word of the LORD is tried" (Ps. 18:30). There is no need to fear where God's Word is concerned because this Scripture clearly says it is a sure foundation on which to build.

The reason I say all of this is the rulers and principalities of this world system are constantly competing for our attention: "There are . . . so many kinds of voices in the world, and none of them is without signification" (1 Cor. 14:10). Each voice we hear has a specific purpose in mind. For example, if the doctor diagnoses you with cancer, the result of that report is to plant doubt in your mind. But is that report the final authority? No! The Word of God is the final authority because only God can produce healing.

A Word from the Lord

At some time in your life, a Christian may come up to you with a "word from the Lord." Honey, put up your antenna because if the Word of God doesn't back it up, it's invalid. Either it is the person's advice (of the flesh), or it is directly from the devil. Proverbs 19:20–21 warns, "Hear counsel, and receive instruction, that thou mayest be wise in thy latter end. There are many devices in a man's heart; nevertheless the counsel of the LORD, that shall stand." Just because a Christian says to you, "I have a word from the Lord," does not necessarily mean that word is from God. You can get into a lot of trouble that way. I've seen people get

> God will always back up what He says with His Word.

married based on a "word from the Lord." Unfortunately, I've seen the same marriages dissolve because God wasn't consulted on the matter. God will *always* back up what He says with His Word. Never accept advice or counsel that is contrary to the Word of God.

"How will I know if it is truly a word from God or a counterfeit?" you may ask. Test the spirit by the spirit. When someone gives you a word from God, it should confirm something that God has already revealed to you. If what the person says doesn't confirm what is in your spirit, it is not of God.

It is vital that we settle this issue in our hearts because too many Christians are jumping off the deep end, allowing anything and everything to be the final authority in their lives. Some would rather take Oprah's advice than God's. The psalmist acknowledged, "For ever, O LORD, thy word is settled in heaven" (Ps. 119:89). God's Word is settled in heaven—but is it settled in your life? A settled issue is a done deal. It is not up for debate or discussion. When the devil comes to attack you, he should encounter the power of God's Word and flee from you, just as he did from Jesus (Luke 4:13). Praise God!

Jesus' Example

Luke 4 describes how Jesus made the Word of God the final authority in His life. Every time the devil tried to tempt or taunt Jesus, He replied by saying, "It is written." Three times the devil attempted to manipulate Jesus, and each time the response was the same: "It is written." Well, the devil wised up. On the fourth try, he said, "If thou be the Son of God, cast thyself down from hence: For it is written, He shall give his angels charge over thee, to keep thee: and in their hands they shall bear thee up, lest at any time thou dash thy foot against a stone" (Luke 4:9–11). The devil responded with the Word of God! But Jesus wasn't fooled. The Bible records,

"And Jesus answering said unto him, It is said, Thou shalt not tempt the Lord thy God" (Luke 4:12).

Jesus knew the Word and used it to avoid Satan's distraction. The Bible says that Satan comes as an angel of light (2 Cor. 11:14). Child of God, unless you decide now to make God's Word the final authority in your life, you will be deceived time and time again. When Satan comes to you with lies, remind him of what *is* written in the Word of God, and send him on his way! You can't afford the luxury of entertaining him. Honey, the last thing you need to do is to have a conversation with the devil. Don't speak anything except what God's Word says. If you resist the devil, he will flee (James 4:7).

The Door to God's Blessing

By choosing to make the Word the final authority in our lives, we open the door to receive the blessings of God. Simon Peter had to learn this the hard way. In the fifth chapter of Luke, Jesus had just finished speaking to a large crowd of followers. He left the crowd and went to Peter, who was nearby. He told Peter, "Launch out into the deep, and let down your nets for a draught" (v. 4). But instead of instantly obeying Jesus, Peter challenged His instructions: "And Simon answering said unto him, Master, we have toiled all the night, and have taken nothing" (v. 5). In other words, Peter said, "Look, Jesus, I've been out here all night fishing, and I don't appreciate Your coming up here and telling me to let down my nets because the fish aren't biting. I really don't see the need to let down the nets again. I've been at this all night, and You've just arrived." But here's the interesting part. Peter, acting as if he were finally willing to obey, let down only one of his nets, although Jesus told him to let down all of them: "Nevertheless at thy word I will let down the net" (v. 5). Read about what happened next:

> And when they had this done, they enclosed a great multitude of fishes: and their net brake. And they beckoned unto their partners, which were in the other ship, that they should come and help them. And they came, and filled both the ships, so that they began to sink. When Simon Peter saw it, he fell down at Jesus' knees, saying, Depart from me; for I am a sinful man, O Lord. (Luke 5:6–8)

They caught so many fish, the net broke! When Peter saw the manifestation of the Word, he felt ashamed. In fact, he felt so low, he told Jesus to go away. Peter allowed the circumstances to cause him to doubt what Jesus said. Because he doubted, he let down only one net when Jesus told him to let down all of them. Therefore, Peter only partially obeyed Jesus.

As my husband teaches, partial obedience is still disobedience. Delayed obedience is disobedience as well.

> *Partial obedience is disobedience.*

When we do only part of what God commands, we disobey. When we delay doing what God instructs us to do, we disobey. The Word of God is true. It will do what it says it will do. If the Word of God promises you something, you can believe that it will come to pass, just as it says, according to your level of faith.

Abraham's wife, Sarah, found it hard to believe the words of the Lord—that she would have a baby in her old age:

> He said, I will certainly return unto thee according to the time of life; and, lo, Sarah thy wife shall have a son. And Sarah heard it in the tent door, which was behind him. Now Abraham and Sarah were old and well stricken in age; and it ceased to be with Sarah after the manner of women. Therefore Sarah laughed within herself, saying, After I am waxed old shall I have pleasure, my lord being old also? And the LORD said unto Abraham, Wherefore did Sarah laugh, saying, Shall I of a surety bear a child, which am old? Is any thing too hard for the LORD? At the time appointed I will return unto thee, according to the time of life, and Sarah shall have a son. (Gen. 18:10–14)

When Sarah heard that she would have a son in her old age, she thought it was a joke. The Bible notes that "it ceased to be with Sarah after the manner of women." Sarah was far past childbearing age, and the idea of a baby was an impossibility for her. Notice I said *for her*. *Anything* is possible with God (Matt. 19:26), and nothing is too hard for Him (Gen. 18:14). True to His word, Sarah gave birth to Isaac.

How many times have you laughed at the promises of God? How many times have you laughed at the biblical teachings on wealth and prosperity? Many of us, at some time or other, have laughed and said, "Man, they've got to be crazy!" For too long tradition and religion have caused us to doubt the validity of the Word of God in spite of the overwhelming evidence.

I remember when Creflo was teaching the congregation about the anointing and how we are able to tap into it. I was amused that he actually believed God would allow us to tap into His anointing. I knew that Creflo was anointed. But I just couldn't envision myself, or anyone who was not a minister, operating in the anointing. So God began to deal with me. He said, "You need to take this teaching seriously." Still I persisted with the idea that I could never be anointed like Creflo.

A few years ago Creflo and I were having lunch in Panama City with some friends—a pastor and his wife. She told me how much of a blessing the women's meeting had been to her. I happened to be one of the speakers at that meeting. She said, "You know, Taffi, you were really anointed." I just looked at her and said, "Psst, child, please! I'm not anointed. I spoke only because of my relationship to you know who." I was referring to my husband. Of course, God dealt with me on that one. He said, "Stop saying that!" I had to change my way of thinking and line it up with the Word of God. God is not a respecter of persons, but He is a respecter of faith. He desires to show Himself strong on behalf of anyone who will completely yield to Him (2 Chron. 16:9).

The Temptation to "Help" God

The real test comes when we don't see the manifestation of our prayers right away. We tend to get discouraged and frustrated if we don't see the fruit of our prayers almost immediately. For Abraham, it meant a 25-year wait for his son Isaac (Gen. 12:4; 13:15–16; 16:2; 21:1–5). Even though the word of the Lord tarried, it eventually came to pass in due season. Now that was a miracle! I mean, that's the kind of stuff we see on the covers of tabloid magazines—the ones with the outrageous headlines that make us laugh.

Do you know that my due season is not your due season? Child of God, understand that due season always comes (Gal. 6:9). No matter how long it takes for the promises of God to manifest, remain patient, consistently obey His Word, and follow His lead.

For too many of us, the temptation to "help" God comes when we see others receiving answers to their prayers before we receive answers to ours. Sarah gave in to this temptation. Even though God told her to expect a son, she became impatient and decided to help Him (Gen. 16:1–4). As a result, Ishmael was born to Abraham through Sarah's maidservant, Hagar, and his descendants have become the enemies of Israel.

God is God all by Himself! He doesn't need your help to bring His promises to pass. If you get involved and try to do things on your own, you'll create trouble. We read in the book of Isaiah, "So shall My word be that goes forth out of My mouth: it shall not return to Me void [without producing any effect, useless], but it shall accomplish that which I please and purpose, and it shall prosper in the thing for which I sent it" (Isa. 55:11 AMPLIFIED). You must believe that God's Word is true, and that He will do exactly what He says.

If God's Word is not the final authority in your life, what is? What have you placed in higher authority? Your friends or family? Maybe the doctor's report? Your financial planner?

In 1 Samuel 9–10, God chose Saul to be king over Israel—a task that he took very seriously at first. But as time passed, Saul began to ignore the counsel of God. For example, God commanded Saul to "utterly destroy the sinners the Amalekites, and fight against them until they be consumed" (1 Sam. 15:18). Instead of obeying God, Saul spared the best of the spoil, including Agag, the Amalekite king. Saul's disobedience angered the Lord, and He sent a message to Saul through His prophet Samuel:

And Samuel came to Saul: and Saul said unto him, Blessed be thou of the LORD: I have performed the commandment of the LORD. And Samuel said, What meaneth then this bleating of the sheep in mine ears, and the lowing of the oxen which I hear? And Saul said, They have brought them from the Amalekites: for the people spared the best of the sheep and of the oxen, to sacrifice unto the LORD thy God; and the rest we have utterly destroyed . . . And Samuel said, Hath the LORD as great delight in burnt offerings and sacrifices, as in obeying the voice of the LORD? Behold, to obey is better than sacrifice, and to hearken than the fat of rams . . . Because thou hast rejected the word of the LORD, he hath also rejected thee from being king. (1 Sam. 15:13–15, 22–23)

As a result of Saul's disobedience, God rejected him as king over Israel and instead crowned David. Saul later committed suicide (1 Sam. 31:4). I don't know about you, but I don't want God to remove His anointing from my life. I don't want Him to regret placing me in the position I am in today. I desire to please God, and I reverence His Word enough to put it first in my life.

> When you trust Him and obey His Word, He will bless and reward you and cause you to have "good success."

It is important that you never do anything to compromise the Word of God. When you trust Him and obey His Word, He will bless and reward you and cause you to have "good success" (Josh. 1:8).

Confession

Heavenly Father, I purpose in my heart right now to make Your Word the final authority in my life. Thank You for bringing all of Your promises to pass in my life. I know that according to Galatians 6:9, I shall reap in due season if I faint not. I thank You for Your Word, and I submit myself to You completely. I declare this to be so now in Jesus' name. Amen.

Study Questions

1. Is the Word of God the final authority in your life? If not, what have you placed in higher authority?

2. How does God confirm what He says to you?

3. Do you base your decisions more on the Word of God or on your past experiences?

4. What happens when you choose to let the Bible be the final authority in your life?

5. Have you ever laughed at something God said to you or tried to help Him when you didn't see results right away?

6. What can you do to avoid getting discouraged and frustrated?

7. How can disobedience to God's Word hinder your walk with Him?

Challenge

Let the Word of God be the final authority in everything you do. In this way, you will have the assurance that all of the promises contained therein will come to pass in your life.

The conclusion of the whole matter: Fear God, and keep his commandments.

—Ecclesiastes 12:13

Conclusion

Everything you need to become a virtuous woman can be found in the Word of God. It is the ultimate source for answers to every life issue. God's Word is His will. Whatever is written in it can not only be done, but should be done. Nothing is too hard for God (Jer. 32:27)!

God's Plan of Operation

Life for many women is a balancing act. Many of us juggle our schedules daily to include work, family, chores, exercise, errands, and more. When God created us, He knew that we would need help in this area. For that reason, He created a standard plan of operation. The plan is that we are to seek His kingdom first and He will provide all the things we need (Matt. 6:32–33). God's *kingdom* is "His way of doing things." Therefore, before we tackle new projects, make decisions,

> *The plan is that we are to seek His kingdom first and He will provide all the things we need.*

or begin our day, we must sit down and spend time with the CEO—God. He has already declared the end from the beginning (Isa. 46:10). He knows how your day will start and end. The same is true of your life.

God has the big picture in view at all times. Where you are right now isn't what matters most; it is where you end up that makes the difference. God is willing to meet you right where you are. That's one of the things I like about God—He doesn't mind U-turns. Wherever you are today, He is willing to meet you. If you've walked away from God's plan in some areas, return to Him.

Many times we condemn ourselves for our mistakes and shortcomings. But John declared, "If we confess our sins, He is faithful and just to forgive us our sins and to cleanse us from all unrighteousness" (1 John 1:9 NKJV). Child of God, once you repent and ask for His forgiveness, let it go! Don't hold on to the extra baggage. Unlike men and women, God will never remind you of your past. Only the devil does that. And when he does, you have the power to shut him down.

There is nothing like walking in the perfect will of God. Knowing the purpose for your life—and living that purpose—is the greatest success achievable. God wants to prosper you, Child of God. He wants you to be successful,

> *God's will doesn't change. It advances level by level.*

healthy, wealthy, and prosperous in all that you do. Before you were born, God established a plan for your life. It's up to you to walk in it.

Ask God to reveal to you His will. Acknowledge Him and He will direct your path (Prov. 3:6). God's will doesn't change. It advances level by level. God's vision for your life may sound overwhelming. On the other hand, it may sound quite simple. Never despise small beginnings. The Word says that although your beginning may be small, your latter end shall greatly increase (Job 8:7).

The ministry that God birthed through my husband had humble beginnings. Initially only eight members attended church services in a school cafeteria. As the vision progressed, we moved into a moderate-size chapel. Now more than twenty thousand members meet in the World Dome weekly. You see, those were levels of growth. Now we're holding meetings and conventions all over the world, and we've opened satellite offices in several foreign countries. God has enabled us to spread the gospel throughout the world via television and radio on the *Changing Your World* broadcast.

"How was all of this done?" you ask. It was accomplished through confessions based on His Word and obedience. God honors obedience, and He is "able to do exceeding abundantly above all that we ask or think, according to the power that worketh in us" (Eph. 3:20).

Remember, you can do all things through Christ (Phil. 4:13). I encourage you to make this Scripture a part of your daily confessions. God honors His Word. And when you make this your confession, He will equip you with the anointing, energy, and resources that you need.

Becoming More Christlike

Tap into the anointing power made available to you daily through the Anointed One and His Anointing— Jesus. As you set your mind to become more Christlike, things will change rapidly. Life as you know it will never be the same again. If you're ready to stretch to the next level in your Christian walk, then "press toward the mark for the prize of the high calling of God in Christ Jesus" (Phil. 3:14). You'll be surprised by how much He will do with your decision to obey and trust Him.

Honor God and He will honor you. Be willing to submit to God's plan and to the established authorities in your life. Remember that submission is for your protection. As you strive to become a virtuous woman, be confident that you are not alone. God is with you. Rest in that.

About the Author

Taffi L. Dollar is the wife of Dr. Creflo A. Dollar Jr. Together they pastor World Changers Church International, a nondenominational, Word-of-Faith church of more than twenty thousand members located in College Park, Georgia. She is the Vice President of World Changers Ministries, the President and CEO of Arrow Records, and the overseer of the Women's Fellowship. An anointed vessel of God, Taffi ministers the gospel of Jesus Christ throughout the country. She can be seen and heard worldwide on the *Changing Your World* radio and television broadcast.

A native of Atlanta, Taffi obtained a bachelor's degree in Mental Health and Human Services from Georgia State University. She accepted Jesus Christ as Lord in 1983 while attending a Bible study lead by Dr. Creflo A. Dollar Jr. on the campus of West Georgia College.

The mother of five, Taffi firmly believes that the best way to raise successful children is to actively demonstrate the divine love and compassion of God found in His Word.

PARTNERSHIP HAS ITS PRIVILEGES

Become a Vision Partner

Our part is to:
- Pray daily that God's blessings be upon you.
- Study the Word and diligently seek God on your behalf.
- Minister to you monthly in a personal letter from Dr. Creflo A. Dollar Jr.
- Provide you with an official partner certificate.
- Periodically offer special gifts for your spiritual edification and growth.

Your part is to:
- Pray for us always.
- Be committed to support meetings in your area.
- Support us financially with your monthly pledge (Phil. 4:17).
- Always lift up the ministry, Dr. Dollar, and his family with positive confessions.

If you would like:
- To order books and tapes by Dr. Creflo A. Dollar Jr.
- To become a partner or supporter of Creflo Dollar Ministries
- To obtain a free copy of the *Changing Your World* magazine

Call us:

United States and Canada 1-888-252-7788

United Kingdom . . . .+44-121-326-9889

Australia . . . .+61-7-5528-1144

South Africa . . . .+27-11-792-5562

Visit our web site: www.worldchangers.org